THE NEW
Altar
Guild
BOOK

THE NEW
Altar
Guild
BOOK

Barbara Gent and Betty Sturges

Morehouse Publishing
NEW YORK · HARRISBURG · DENVER

Morehouse Publishing, 4775 Linglestown Road, Harrisburg, PA 17112
Morehouse Publishing, 445 Fifth Avenue, New York, NY 10016

Morehouse Publishing is an imprint of Church Publishing Incorporated.

Library of Congress Cataloging-in-Publication Data
Gent, Barbara.
    [Altar guild book]
    The new altar guild book / Barbara Gent. Betty Sturges.
        p. cm.
        Originally published : The altar guild book. Wilton, Conn. : Morehouse-
Barlow, c. 1982.
        Includes bibliographical references.
        ISBN 0-8192-1657-7 (pbk.)
        1. Altar guild—Episcopal Church—Handbooks, manuals, etc. 2. Episcopal
Church—Liturgy—Handbooks, manuals, etc. 3. Anglican Communion—
Liturgy—Handbooks, manuals, etc. I. Sturges, Betty. II. Title.
BX5948.G46 1996
247—dc20   98-5655

Contents

Foreword

$\mathcal{H}$ealthy liturgy depends on a hidden network of preparation by liturgists, musicians, lectors, preachers, intercessors, acolytes, ushers, oblation bearers, eucharistic ministers, and — not least — altar guilds. Yet, unlike most of the others who contribute to the liturgy, those responsible for the tangible and visible parts of worship are seldom recognized for what they do. Other people wear the vestments they make and care for, or offer the bread and wine they provide. And other people can carelessly spill things on the linens they have spent hours washing and ironing, or knock over flowers they have carefully arranged, or drip rivers of wax down the brass candlesticks they have laboriously polished. While others who contribute to liturgy appear to have lively and varied ministries, the altar guild often seems restricted to dull and repetitive tasks: wash and iron this, polish that, order more of something else, and then do it all again.

Part of the good news contained in this book (and made even clearer in this new edition) is liberation for the slaves in the sacristy. There will always be necessary preparations to make, of course; but they need not be the burden of only a faithful few. Engaging a wider spectrum of the worshiping community (including men and children) can dispel the erroneous but lingering perception that these matters are only "women's work" and probably ought to be borne in semi-penitential silence.

As a careful reading of these pages will make clear, the full ministry of those who care for a liturgical space extends far beyond the merely functional duties customarily associated with altar guilds. Especially when this ministry is appreciated as an extension of a truly creative and incarnational faith, responsibility for preparing a place for worship implies careful attention to all the furnishings and decorations in the space where worshipers gather. Although there will always be some obligation to act as curators of the accumulated strata of vessels, linens, furniture and vestments handed down by previous generations, the primary focus of their efforts needs to be the worship of those who gather here and now.

In the chapters that follow, Barbara Gent and Betty Sturges offer a lively blend of liturgical history, sacramental theology, and practical hints to assist people concerned with preparing a place for worship, whether the space be established or temporary. By principle and example they equip attentive readers to deal with the special challenges arising in their own situations. Yet, for all its information and practical advice, this book is not an answer book so much as it is a guide to asking important questions. In countless ways the authors effectively illustrate how to determine what is essential, possible, or desirable.

What is essential?

No small part of the power of Good Friday liturgies is the experience of the worship space reduced to the starkness of its essential furnishings. The absence of ornament underscores the primacy of what remains; it is also a benchmark against which any additions must be measured. In particular, the three liturgical centers — font, table, lectern/pulpit — need to be prominent and visible. Decoration alone cannot compensate for poor placement or inappropriate size. Nor is it good stewardship to continue to buy and maintain hangings, linens and vessels designed for inherited furnishings that do not exemplify the faith we claim to profess: diminutive fonts that trivialize Baptism, monumental altars that preclude any sense of gathering about the Lord's Table, and separate lecterns and pulpits that divide the proclamation of the Word.

Everything added to these three fundamental centers articulates their significance or facilitates the action taking place there: a ewer for pouring water into the font, tables or shelves for vessels used at the altar, a Bible or books containing the readings, and so on through all the practical requirements of equipping and preparing a space for worship.

What is possible?

How refreshing it is to learn that many presumed limitations have been arbitrary and unnecessary! Vestments and hangings need not be limited to four or five so-called liturgical colors. Vessels and furnishings do not have to be made of silver or brass, nor must they come from a church supply house. Flowers from the garden or the roadside are not inferior offerings. In short, many of the well-intentioned rules of past generations are shown to be needless restrictions. Instead of "thou shalt not" the watchwords become "what if?" In numerous ways the authors reiterate the practical and ethical obligation to discover what is appropriate for each worshiping community and the place(s) where that congregation gathers — and to do so with a spirit of celebrating the uniqueness of each situation rather than lamenting how it may fall short of some perceived ideal. A small wood-framed church is not a soaring stone cathedral and need not pretend to be, but its more intimate scale permits it to do things a larger space could never attempt.

What is desirable?

Between the firmness of the essential and the freedom of the possible lies the variable middle ground of the desirable. What will most effectively enhance worship for this congregation in this place and time? If ornaments and furnishings leave no visual or aural space for worshipers (e.g. elaborate wall decorations or sound-swallowing carpet) or compete for attention with the three primary foci (e.g. a dazzling stained glass window or an overlarge cross), they can run the risk of becoming an end rather than a means. One reliable rule of thumb is that a good liturgical space simultaneously seems incomplete without people yet fosters an awareness of the mystery of God. Another important criterion is that anything in the worship space which cannot be altered either in appearance or placement runs the risk of becoming an idol. Especially as a worshiping community moves through the seasons and the feasts of the liturgical calendar, there should be clear visual, tactile, and spatial reinforcement for the changes from, say, Epiphany to Lent to Holy Week to Easter.

In the pages that follow, Barbara Gent and Betty Sturges share abundantly from their knowledge, experience, enthusiasm, and sheer love for the ministry of preparing a place where people can worship. They provide a book that is fascinating to read through as well as one that can be consulted as a reference work or as a guide to specialized studies. Above all they communicate the vitality and the joy of this ministry.

Carl P. Daw, Jr.

CHAPTER 1

To Begin With...

*I*n 1979, when we were writing the first edition of *The Altar Guild Book*, the Episcopal Church was just becoming used to the new hardcover *Book of Common Prayer*. Changes that had been predicted through the years of paperback trial services had become reality, and all of us Episcopalians were involved in thinking about our primary work as the People of God: our prayer life together. We were experiencing liturgical renewal firsthand. By the time *The Altar Guild Book* was published three years later, innovation in our worship life was more or less the norm everywhere. Shifts in our words and practices and in the ornaments and furnishings of our churches, although often unsettling and sometimes unwelcome, no longer surprised us. And along the way, of course, many familiar objects, many of the ceremonies that we had grown up with, were slipping out of sight.

Now, fifteen years later, it is difficult to recapture the sense of loss, almost of betrayal, that many church people felt when confronted for the first time by change in this most fundamental part of life—the way we say our prayers. The feeling was there, nevertheless, especially among altar guild members. Therefore in writing *The New Altar Guild Book* we tried to move gently along the path away from the old altar guild manuals filled with specific directions about how to do everything. Those directions had become irrelevant, even confusing. We described some alternative practices and paraphernalia of worship already in place in many localities. We recounted a little history tracing some new practices back to the church of the early centuries and showing that many of the old practices now gone had been around for less than a hundred years—that "the new liturgy" was far from new. We indicated the range of possibilities open to people preparing places for worship, encouraging altar guilds to follow their best instincts in going about their work. And we repeatedly suggested that priests and altar guilds work together to write their own altar guild manuals, local

1

manuals that could be adjusted to keep up with changes that were destined to come in parish liturgical life.

Many altar guild members and some priests struggled with the idea that worship today is meant to be as free an expression of people's thankfulness to God as it was in the second century. They had trouble understanding that the worship life of a whole parish (and the preparation for it) could be tailored to fit its circumstances just as readily as an individual's could. Writing parish manuals, putting into print "the way we do it," was an almost overwhelming thought to some. It felt like stepping out of line, trespassing on sacred ground. But fifteen years later hundreds of parish manuals have been written. And because the new adventure in worship has challenged the imagination of people in parishes as well as liturgists at large, many of these parish manuals have already been *re*written! They differ in content, as widely as people differ. They differ in format, some directing each action in minute detail, others allowing for continuing creativity. Guides to preparing for special services such as weddings, the Easter Vigil, Great Festival Eucharists, and Baptism are just as varied. The work of worship obviously doesn't adhere to a pattern! Actually it never did.

Most altar guild members today are relatively comfortable with the changes that have taken place. Most are now open to imaginative thinking about liturgy both for their own parishes and for the church in other places. They know it is "all right" to make unusual vestments and linens, to bake "real" bread for the Eucharist and brew the wine, to grow and arrange their own altar flowers, to beautify their sacred spaces according to their own sense of good taste. Many now serve on parish liturgical committees and participate in planning worship for their communities. In other words, they know that with very few restrictions they are now in fact free to experience the true joy of worship.

In our 1982 preface we said,

> Our stint in the altar guild ministry in the last forty years (now over fifty) has been a double journey. We both have traveled the path from the strict training in altar guild procedures of the forties through the confusion of that training in the fifties by variations in ceremonial and by the trial services. We both have also had the privilege of worshiping in Episcopal churches throughout this country. Our own lives have taken us into churches north, south,

2

east, and west and into [diocesan and national] altar guild responsibilities. Our worship away from home has been a boon because altar guild background, like background in any other discipline, sharpens the eye and the ear to the familiar [and the unfamiliar] and we have grown in our understanding of liturgy because of it.

And our journey continues today. We have been blessed from our first steps in this ministry by excellent teachers in person and in print, and we continue to be. Men and women, priests, laypeople, artists in various media—a list would go on and on. A compendium of what we have learned from them would be, in effect, a wide-ranging course in liturgy. They have alerted us to the countless ways of "doing" our worship and of preparing for it, and to the importance of telling altar guilds what we have learned. Today in this ministry we are bound by just a few rubrics in *The Book of Common Prayer.* Except for those and for guidance by our parish priests,[1] we are truly free to use our own ingenuity as we prepare for the parish liturgy.

In rewriting *The Altar Guild Book* for this new day, we examined the pages one by one with an eye alert to where we are now in this ministry and with an ear tuned to the suggestions we have received from readers. As a result, we have retained some material and dropped some as no longer pertinent. We have moved some to the appendix on its way into history and added some because of new practices adopted or new products developed. And because our readers have supported our belief that knowing liturgical history keeps us aware of what we are about in our altar guild work, we have woven into this revision more background of the furnishings of worship than was included in the original edition.

The New Altar Guild Book

*T*he *New Altar Guild Book* is designed to provide background material for altar guild members old and new and for anyone else assigned to prepare church buildings and altars for worship. It is an information book, a general guidebook, not an old-style manual. Manuals laid out an inherited "standard procedure" that the liturgical studies of the mid-twentieth century have shown to be largely custom, at times adhered to and at other times not. Through the years most ceremonial practices and the preparation for them have depended on local circumstances, have become "standard," and then have changed as the world has changed. There have been many types of buildings in which to worship, many ways to conduct worship, many kinds of vessels, vestments, linens, and other church furnishings to use in worship, and many ways to prepare them for that use. All have been acceptable in their time and place, and all have gone through change that was disruptive in its day. This sentence buried in the pages of Gregory Dix's extensive study of liturgy written in the early twentieth century would be a reassuring insert for every parish altar guild manual: "What preposterous nonsense it is to try to erect sacristy orthodoxies and even tests of theological allegiance out of minute details of pious furnishings that have varied endlessly throughout Christian history and have never meant anything in particular by all their changes!"[2]

Worship, as Christians understand it, is a thank-offering to God for their lives because God sent Jesus Christ to redeem those lives. Christians worship on their own time and in their own ways as individuals, but when they gather as members of the Body of Christ to give thanks together and in community to celebrate their redemption, the community becomes a new individual. The community life is a composite of the lives that shape it, and its liturgy expresses that life with its own individuality.

The Book of Common Prayer supports that individuality by allowing variation in worship within a few guidelines set by the rubrics.

When worship varies, preparation for it also varies as widely as the circumstances, talents, resources, and imaginations of each worshiping community. Uniformity is in the central act of each sacrament, not in the manner of its performance. To assure that uniformity, some Prayer Book rubrics are binding, but most are now permissive, suggestive, to welcome variety. Each worshiping group today is free to express its own nature, its own personality, in most of its ceremonial. As a result, liturgy can differ, not only from parish to parish, but within each parish as well, from week to week, season to season, year to year.

"Standard procedure" with its "shoulds" and "musts," its emphasis on "proper" and "correct," doesn't make room for much individuality. The old familiar manuals limit the offering of talent that altar guild members in each community make through their work. They restrict the joy of preparing places for Easter and Pentecost and Christmas and all the other days. Even with updating and local editing, they can't provide enough material to guide all altar guilds everywhere through the intricacies of making their different places ready for all services of worship. No general manual could encompass all the patterns!

With their new freedom, altar guild workers have an increased responsibility, and so do priests. Those who prepare places for worship need more information than they did when they could depend on general manuals to guide their every move. In order to do what they are now called to do, it is important for them to learn at least something about the history of sacraments and other worship traditions. They need to be thoroughly familiar with their own situations—with their priests' ideas, with their fellow parishioners' attitudes, and with their own resources of time, talent, equipment, and money. They also need to stay abreast of the constant changes in art, technology, society, and the economy in respect to the ways all four affect the many aspects of their work. And they have to find answers to new questions that stem from new ideas, new products, and new challenges in all these areas.

Today people who prepare church buildings for worship really benefit when they have local manuals to work with, guidebooks to all aspects of altar guild work in their own parishes. They need manuals that can be revised and updated easily and regularly as conditions (and priests) change. In order to produce these manuals they need information not only about their parish traditions but also about today's developments in the church at large, both liturgically and practically. They acquire this kind of information from their priests, from observation, from experience, and from books.

The New Altar Guild Book is a book to start with. It looks at the altar guild ministry as a whole, its background, its purpose, its varied structure. The book includes material about vestments and vessels, linens and hangings, flowers and candles, bread and wine, housekeeping and preparation for worship. It recalls the church's yesterdays and speaks to its today. Interspersed throughout the text are page references to rubrics in *The Book of Common Prayer* that affect altar guild work. Books used as reference for preparing the text are listed in the bibliography, and several other titles for further reference are listed in appropriate sections. *The New Altar Guild Book* is intended to help parish altar guilds create their own manuals, providing enough information for that purpose.

A half-century ago John Baillie wrote a prayer that speaks clearly to altar guilds today:

> Give me an open mind, O God, a mind ready to receive and to welcome such new light of knowledge as it is thy will to reveal to me. Let not the past ever be so dear to me as to set a limit to the future. Give me courage to change my mind, when that is needed. Let me be tolerant to the thoughts of others and hospitable to such light as may come to me through them. Amen.[3]

CHAPTER 2

Yesterday and Today

ORIGINS OF THE ALTAR GUILD MINISTRY

ltar guilds, as the Episcopal Church has known them, developed in the late nineteenth century, a natural outgrowth of what had been from the beginning an exclusively male world. In the early days of the church, when followers of Christ gathered in private homes to break bread together and share their memories of him, presumably the head of the household provided whatever was required for the meal. As Christians multiplied and needed larger buildings in which to meet, certain people were given the task of caring for these places, and the worshipers themselves provided the food for the meal (and for their leaders and the poor besides). By the fourth century something like the parochial ministry of today, a "local Christian family," had become more or less established. For hundreds of years thereafter certain leaders (later called clerics, then sacristans) were responsible for everything that is now considered "altar guild work." A sacristan supervised the sacristy and all the paraphernalia of worship, prepared for services, and did the church housekeeping as well.

In the early days of the Church of England, altar care was also the task of clerics—the sacristan and the verger in a cathedral and clerks in parishes. Years later, laymen became the sacristans, and eventually women were included in this ministry. Percy Dearmer's words about the duties of the sacristan ("who had much better be a layman") written about 1900 tell the altar guild story for both England and the United States at that time.

> The sacristan's position is a most important one, and he must be devout, sensible, and even-tempered...He need not do a very great deal himself, but he must see that everything is done, which means that he must be kind and pleasant in manner as well as careful. He should have a general knowledge of the matters he has to deal with...He will see that a list of servers is posted on the wall for every

service in the week...He will see that everything is ready five minutes before service begins on Sunday—the vestments laid out, the candles lit by a taperer, and the charcoal heated by the thurifer. He will gently superintend the band of helpers who are needed if everything is to be kept as the things pertaining to God's worship ought to be kept. For many duties women are best, only they need to have their realms well-defined and protected, and unless they are responsible to the sacristan there may sometimes be trouble...A lady will often be needed to put out (the server's) vestments every day, and her work will require much neatness of method. She may also be responsible for mending and washing the albes, etc., of clergy and servers. Another may be needed to polish the brass work and to trim the candles...(a lad may clean the brass and other metal but women are more reliable, and men cannot generally spare sufficient time). Another may be needed to dust the high altar and see to the altar cloths, and another to see to the chapel. Often another lady...can undertake the useful task of washing the purificators...If there are several helpers, each responsible for his or her own piece of work, and all are responsible to the Sacristan, and through him to the Parson, the most perfect cleanliness and order can be secured...[4]

Sometime in the nineteenth century women did become assistants to sacristans, at least in the English part of the church. By the turn of the twentieth century they were beginning to organize into guilds, and in most places in the United States these "altar guilds" assumed the sacristan's duties themselves under the guidance of their priests. Since then, in the Episcopal Church, women have predominated in altar guilds, perhaps because until 1970 this channel was the only route open to them for serving God in the sanctuary. It has become apparent, however, that men can be as helpful to women in altar guilds as women once were to the men in Percy Dearmer's sacristy. Now at the end of the twentieth century men are taking part in this ministry in increasing numbers. They serve as sacristans, designers, craftsmen, flower arrangers, embroiderers, candle makers, needlepointers, and just plain keepers of the house of the Lord. Once again the care and decoration of the church in preparation for worship is becoming a joint lay ministry.

In several churches today this joint lay ministry extends beyond the bounds of a formal altar guild organization, and preparation for worship has become the responsibility of the parish family. Small groups from the worshiping community (family units, for example, parents and children together) carry out all the tasks traditionally done by altar guilds before a service. They are trained and work on a regular basis (each group for a month at a time perhaps) cleaning, readying the worship centers and things of worship, even supplying (sometimes making) the bread and the wine. In some churches special groups are responsible for special occasions (weddings, funerals, Christmas) or special tasks (laundry, flowers, repairs). But in most churches the basic group shares all the work.

The "parish family" method of altar care also appears in various kinds of institutions: summer camps, retirement homes, hospitals, prisons, conference centers, religious houses, and the like. In these places members of the community (residents and staff) are often those charged with the care and preparation of the altar for services. In all these circumstances that involve people not formally organized as altar guilds, guidelines worked out by the priest-in-charge for each specific situation are indispensible if the preparation for worship is to run smoothly and easily and be "a joyful offering to the Lord."

Although the term *altar guild* is used all through this book because it is the familiar one for this special ministry in the church, the material in the book is intended for any group engaged in caring for an altar and its furnishings and in making any place ready for worship.

TRANSITION

The difficulty some altar guild members have today with changes in their familiar routine comes from their almost too strict training yesterday in a procedure that was itself the result of changes that altar guilds faced in another era. In the days of Percy Dearmer's women assistants to the sacristan, the women's work was primarily housekeeping—special housekeeping with some unusual tasks, but housekeeping nevertheless. Preparation for the rites and ceremonies of the church was the sacristan's assignment and that of his male helpers. What he needed was assistance in keeping the building and its furnishings "decent and in order."

This situation had not changed appreciably when women first banded into altar guilds in the United States. Then, toward the end of the nineteenth century in some areas, later in others, "seasonal colors" and historic eucharistic vestments started to appear for the first time in the Episcopal Church.[5] In this same period the clergy in many parishes began to encourage more frequent services of Holy Communion than the monthly or quarterly celebrations then customary. They also started to add bits of ceremonial historically attached to that rite by including lavabo, incense, bells, and the like. Altar guilds found they had to learn many things in order to do whatever had to be done to prepare their churches for the new departures in worship.

At first they learned from their priests, later from little handbooks written especially for them, filled with precise details about each aspect of preparation. They learned terms, routines, and historic customs as well as taboos and allegories. They learned what was then known or supposed about rites and ceremonial, and they found their work expanding far beyond the tasks of simple housekeeping. They learned to dress the altar, set the credence, prepare the chalice, lay out the vestments, make the linens and launder them in specific ways, arrange flowers, and place and light candles, following directions presented as if there were only one way to do these things. One exact way.

To be sure, different priests had their own methods of teaching altar guilds, and they weren't exactly alike. The little handbooks were written by different individuals, so they, too, weren't exactly alike. Here and there the altar guild procedure in a parish was adapted to fit a local situation and the adaptation was perhaps copied by neighbors. Nevertheless, in spite of these variations, altar guild training was basically uniform. It bred women devoted to the altar guild ministry and produced altar guilds with a common understanding of what was expected of them. Parishes may have differed in specific practices, but altar guilds usually were not alert to those differences because manuals didn't acknowledge them and people generally worshiped in their own parishes. In fact, altar guild members became so conscientious about adhering meticulously to what they had been taught that they assumed a "right way" that didn't exist and considered deviations from it "wrong." Any kind of change in their work was inconceivable to them.

Change happens though, in the church as in the rest of life, and in the church it is just as difficult to adjust to as elsewhere. Intense training for nearly a century in a single way of preparing a church building for worship (the Eucharist or any other service) compounded the problem for altar guilds faced in 1979 with the changing liturgy of *The Book of Common Prayer*. The uncertainties of that earlier time of changing rites and ceremonies had been forgotten because the customs introduced in those years had for so long been the status quo. The idea that worship practices had varied, could vary, from age to age and place to place was contradictory to traditional altar guild thinking and experience. It is, however, a historical reality.

Today, in this time of the church, that reality is at the heart of altar guild instruction. New liturgical insight has made many familiar old words and ceremonies of the first part of the twentieth century redundant because ideas and practices that are far older in the church have been brought back into the liturgy. New world conditions have presented new situations and new problems to which old customs do not speak. New techniques challenge old practices, new inventions raise questions about the efficiency of old products. But new is neither right nor wrong: it is just new. In former ages the church incorporated the new of its time into its liturgy, giving it place beside the old or instead of the old. Today the church does the same. It will do so tomorrow. There is space for both Gothic and A-frame, for an altar on the east wall and an altar in the nave, for brocade and polyester, silver and earthenware. Whether the bread and the wine are homemade or not, the Lord Jesus comes, and whether the People of God stand or kneel, they receive him with thanksgiving.

Generally Speaking about Altar Guilds

Altar guilds today are groups of men and women who are called to serve God by preparing and tending the places where Episcopalians worship. They are organized in different ways, but wherever they are, the work they do together is an offering of time and many talents. It is a ministry of love undertaken in the name of Christ.

Altar guild work goes on quietly behind the scenes. The work is often not noticed because in normal circumstances average worshipers don't think about the familiar scene in front of them as long as it *is* familiar. They don't consider who has put the ornaments and furnishings in place or who cares for them. Yet these two responsibilities have been fundamental to the altar guild ministry from its start. Some altar guilds do very little else. Some shoulder a wide range of other responsibilities, such as making or purchasing vestments and linens; managing flower monies and orders as well as arranging the flowers; replenishing (even making) the supply of bread, wine, and candles; creating objects of art of various kinds for use or decoration; teaching church school classes, acolytes, or other groups about the things of worship; suggesting memorial gifts for use in the church; participating in special ceremonies such as stripping the altar on Maundy Thursday. What altar guilds are asked to do, how they are organized in the first place, depends on the priest for whom they work.

Unlike most other parish organizations, an altar guild is not intended to be involved in parish business or social matters; it has a special role as the priest's liturgical partner in making the worship life of the parish run smoothly. Because of this responsibility, selection of people to prepare the altar is a thoughtful process. Their part in the parish liturgical life is vital, and their good working relationship with the priest is important. Altar guild work is truly a vocation: workers are "called" to it. Their response indicates a willingness, as Bishop Appleton Lawrence said years ago, "to give more of their time and of themselves than is usually asked by the Church."[6] Talent and know-how are always useful attributes for altar guild members, but loyalty and commitment are indispensible if the priest is to lead the parish in worship with equanimity.

If a priest wishes to have a traditional altar guild care for equipment and prepare for services, that priest appoints the members and is the head of the guild. Typically the priest selects a suitable person, man or woman, to oversee the work. (This person has been variously titled directress or director, coordinator, sacristan, or president.) The priest arranges for other officers or committee heads when the situation warrants and arranges for members to be instructed carefully in all aspects of the work they are expected to do.

A traditional altar guild is not the only answer to altar care and preparation in a parish, however. A priest may very well choose to follow some other practice. A priest may even decide in the midst of tenure to change from one kind of altar guild to another. If this situation arises in a parish, an established altar guild may need to be reminded that it exists only because the priest has invited it to and its ministry in the sanctuary is determined only by the priest's need for it.

The corollary of all this is that no group of people caring for the altar in a parish is meant to go on forever, least of all an altar guild leader. All successive priests have the privilege of making their own appointments and arranging for the care of the altar and the preparation for worship in their parishes. Bishop Lawrence, again: "It should be recognized by altar guild members that there is of necessity a variety of tradition, custom, and practice within our Church; and the wishes of one rector may be very different from those of another. The present rector's orders are 'the orders of the day.'"[7] So although a new priest in a parish may find an "inherited altar guild leader" and an "inherited guild" to be adaptable and cooperative (or an inherited "other practice" working successfully), it is customary for all to resign (or to be ready to resign when convenient) to enable the new priest to select a new group—or not to select one, if that seems preferable.

Altar guild organization has to be a local matter because each parish situation is different. Some altar guilds have only one worker; some, as many as fifty; some aim to involve the entire parish family. Some divide tasks according to expertise; some share them equally. Some prepare for worship in teams of two to five or more; some, individually. Some assign duty for a month at a time; some, for a week. Some hold regular meetings for planning, instruction, and fellowship; some meet infrequently. Responsibilities vary widely from parish to parish, as do working conditions and the time, talent, and resources of workers. It might be convenient to pretend that all altar guilds fit into one organizational mold, but it is unrealistic.

Nevertheless organization of some kind is important for altar guilds just as it is for any other group that shares a continuing charge with exacting details. Some system has to be devised in each parish to assure that preparation for every worship occasion will be completed on time according to the priest's wishes. Working out such a system and implementing it is a leader/priest responsibility. In so doing, it is helpful for both to keep in mind that an altar guild

15

"works together separately" and produces dependable results only when the separate units are given detailed instructions. Each parish altar guild needs adequate guidelines for its own procedure. It needs a schedule tailored to its workers' available time because today most of them have other obligations. It needs thoughtful assignment of special tasks with consideration given to workers' enthusiasms and talents. It needs careful instruction for new participants, regular review for older participants, and constant updating for all to keep abreast of changes. The group also needs opportunities for all workers to meet as a whole in order to build a sense of the togetherness that gives them their reason for working separately. Meeting regularly in "fellowship, in the breaking of bread and in the prayers" (*The Book of Common Prayer*, hereafter *BCP*, p. 304) deepens the bond of shared ministry.

The bond among altar guild members extends beyond the parish through the ministry of larger altar guild organizations—diocesan, provincial, and national. The primary purpose of all these groups is to support parish altar guilds by serving as resource centers for them. All three relay pertinent information; open up opportunities for learning about subjects related to altar work by means of conferences, meetings, publications, and program materials; and encourage and facilitate the redistribution of used ecclesiastical furnishings. (For further information, see Appendix 1.) As changes in liturgy and in the world catapult parish altar guilds into successive tomorrows, the purpose of these larger groups will become increasingly meaningful. Invariably, a question in one parish has been answered in another somewhere, and through exchanging information parish to parish, diocese to diocese, across the country, it is possible for questions and answers to meet. Apart from all their other projects, the national, provincial, and diocesan altar guilds serve parishes well with an efficient communications network.

THE WORK ROOM OF AN ALTAR GUILD

A sacristy is a room in a church or parish house where vestments, hangings, linens, vessels, and other furnishings and housekeeping equipment used by altar guilds are kept. As its name indicates, it also is sacred space. Most parish churches have a working sacristy, thoughtfully planned or makeshift, large or small. Some churches have a priest's sacristy (vestry, vesting room) as well. If a sacristy is especially small, some room or closet elsewhere in the church may have to become a second sacristy. If there is no adequate space for any working sacristy, altar guild members are challenged to prepare for Eucharists and other services and care for altar equipment in whatever dignified way they can without one. Many ingenious sacristies have been created by distraught altar guilds seeking a room of their own!

No two working sacristies are alike, but all share the common characteristic of providing as efficient a center for church housekeeping as possible and having as many closets, drawers, and shelves as space allows. To describe particularly practical types of storage (adjustable shelves, shallow drawers, divided closets) is useful primarily for parishes designing new sacristies or redoing old ones, but improvising storage spaces (open shallow boxes, for example) to accommodate the shapes and sizes of the items to be stored can be extremely helpful in any sacristy. It is important that valuable objects be kept secure in a safe when not in use, although locating the safe in the sacristy is not necessary. Careful plans can make a sacristy as useful and pleasant to work in as a well-designed kitchen. Suggestions for practical ways to store linens, hangings, and vestments are included in sections about those items. A full description of a useful working sacristy is included in Appendix 2.

If an altar guild surveys the tasks it is expected to do and the possessions it has to store, it will soon discern how best to use its available space. Each group has to work out its own plan. The most important precept for it to keep in mind is that no sacristy design is final. Even though an ideal sacristy has a storage space labeled for every item in current use, no space belongs forever to the item stored in it. Storage spaces can always be reassigned or redesigned as parish needs and equipment change.

PREPARING A PLACE FOR WORSHIP

Altar guild workers prepare for all worship services, including Morning and Evening Prayer and the other Offices as well as all the sacramental rites. The Sunday Eucharist, however, is the service that involves the greatest effort and the most knowledge. If the other services take place by themselves, they require minimal preparation beyond making the church ready, and they call for very little equipment—a baptismal bowl, a funeral pall, wedding kneelers, flowers, candles, a few vestments. But *The Book of Common Prayer* is eucharistically centered, and the Eucharist is written so that it can encompass these other services as the "Liturgy of the Word." If they are conducted in this way, preparing for them becomes part of the greater preparation for the Eucharist itself.

The Eucharist is not a last minute happening. It is "the principal act of Christian worship on the Lord's Day" (*BCP*, p. 13) and increasingly on most other occasions when Episcopalians gather to worship. The People of God are all preparing for it every day of their lives. In addition, some people make special preparations in order for it to happen each time. Whether a service is to be in the church building or away from it, bakers and winemakers, artisans and artists, vestry and sexton, choir and secretary, priest and altar guild, all have tasks to do well before the appointed hour. The altar guild prepares the place.

Preparing a place for the Eucharist is preparing a place for a family celebration. Cleaning the house; decorating suitably with flowers, candles, and hangings to honor the special guest; setting the table with the best linens and dishes; dressing up; putting out the dishes and the food: all these acts are steps in preparing for any festive meal. Each familiar act gains special significance before the Great Festival where Christ comes to be with his followers in the Breaking of the Bread. The whole task of getting ready acquires overtones of holiness.

To make Eucharist, after the lessons and prayers are read, worshipers may just gather around a plain wooden table (or a similar flat surface) with no covering except a clean white cloth and no ornaments. They may give the presider bread enough to share, some wine in a bottle, and a cup large enough for the group. The presider places these gifts on the cloth. Then the Liturgy of the Table can begin. Relatively little preparation is needed for such a simple meal.

Altar guild workers build from that base in preparing any place for the Eucharist. They bring their symbols of joy and light and beauty and freedom to turn the simple meal into a feast of thanksgiving. The rubrics of the Eucharist require a table spread with a clean white cloth during the celebration, bread, wine, a little water, and a cup. That's all. The other rubrics for the Eucharist that refer to church furnishings are suggestive, not binding, worded with "it is desirable," "it is appropriate," and "may." Whatever else altar guild workers add to prepare for each occasion, they add with the permission of their priest, either acting on their own initiative or possibly following suggestions of a parish liturgical committee. Options are as diverse as talent, imagination, resources, and good taste allow.

In most cases the place for worship is already "there," and an altar guild's additions and rearrangements have to be within that framework. Additions may be traditional or contemporary, old or new, practical or decorative, simple or ornate. If whatever is added becomes part of the whole place and beautifies it, fits the occasion, adds to the service, and doesn't distract the worshiping group, it is suitable. The point is to intensify the worship experience, not to interrupt it.

It is important for everyone concerned to know that things do not have to be formally dedicated to God to be used in a church. Temporary hangings, vessels, linens, and vestments; impromptu candle and flower holders; even quite ordinary tables serving as substitute altars can be suitable for the liturgy. They become suitable when they are endowed with their new church purpose by being carefully put in place for a time.

The way altar guild workers perform their tasks is crucial to their ministry. Their commitment is to serving the Lord, not to getting a job done. In "preparing the place" their concern is to create a setting for worship that is as complete as they can possibly make it, using the time and talents and resources they have been given to create a setting that is "whole." Because wholeness is related to holiness, to spiritual health, their first step is to detach themselves from their own busy worlds for a time and offer their hands and their thoughts to God. Then they proceed to cleaning and decorating. They are careful about details of housekeeping, more so than they would ordinarily be in their own homes. They are as gentle with the things they touch as if these were their own precious treasures. They are considerate of each other's contributions to the work, as they hope others will be of theirs. They are willing to give as much time as it takes to do what has to be done.

A gentle touch for the ornaments of worship is important, but there is a pitfall. At the outset of their service, altar guild workers learn to handle these objects gently because of their value, real and sentimental. They may be made of fine materials and represent great initial expense. They may be erstwhile gifts and very old. They

19

may be difficult to replace if damaged. Like all lovely things, therefore, they will last longer if they are treated well. As a rule most ornaments of worship have also been set aside for the liturgical life of the parish, dedicated in prayer for use at the altar. This dedication of things "to the glory of God" can easily become confused with actual godliness and sometimes is. The line between the objects and their purpose may become clouded, and people may begin to think of them as "holy," refer to them as "holy." But objects are not holy in themselves. If they are handled gently, reverently, by people who are dedicated to serving God through this ministry, if in other words, they are handled in a holy way, they may thereby be touched with holiness. Without that extra ingredient in the care given them, the valuable objects of the church are just valuable objects.

The place, too. The place that an altar guild prepares for worship is just a place unless the people preparing it center their work in God. When they work deliberately, reverently, filled with joy in what they are doing, they work in a holy way. They preserve the atmosphere of God's presence in an old church, and they bring his presence into a new place of worship, even a temporary place, by focusing on its purpose. They touch it with holiness.

CLEANING THE HOUSE

Cleaning is the first step in preparing a place for the Eucharist or any other service of worship: cleaning the sanctuary and chancel, the other worship centers of the church building, and the sacristy. Even temporary worship places such as halls, informal outdoor chapels, and sick rooms need to be neat and orderly before being used for worship. The goal of good church housekeeping is a neat, clean house.

In general, altar guild workers sweep and dust, scrub and shine, trim and straighten, using their combined know-how to do their assigned tasks well. Some altar guilds have full care of the worship centers of the church; some are assisted by the sexton/verger and occasionally by professional cleaning people. Some work in teams and share all the housekeeping chores equitably each time they work. Others assign housekeeping chores on a regular basis to specific persons, often by request, leaving only the sacristan duties to be shared before a service. Some altar guilds schedule special sessions for special tasks such as polishing silver, brass, and wood; mending linens and vestments; cleaning and inventorying the sacristy; or doing other time-consuming and infrequent jobs that are accomplished pleasantly in fellowship and quickly when many hands share the work. While working, some altar guilds wear smocks or aprons (even head coverings) for protection and for the anonymity that uniforms bestow.

Most altar guild workers are aware of the fund of information about housekeeping (stain removal, metal and wood care, for example) that is readily available from books, government pamphlets, and the files of diocesan altar guilds. "Hints for homemakers" are also hints for church housekeepers. Several suggestions for the care of specific church furnishings (candles, vessels, linens, vestments) are incorporated into the appropriate sections of this book. Appendix 4 contains a few suggestions for removing stains.

Each altar guild has to establish its own housekeeping system and its own work schedule. Each also has to make up its own list of cleaning tasks to be done for each worship occasion, determined by the place it is making ready and the priest with whom it works. No two churches have identical equipment or staff, and no two altar guilds approach identical sets of tasks. A standard list of cleaning procedures for everyone is therefore pointless. Any system is acceptable for a particular parish as long as all the workers in that parish understand what is to be done before each service and how the assignment is to be carried out. Any system is acceptable as long as it works well and the place benefits by it. Neatness and cleanliness come first; decorating, setting the table, and preparing the vestments follow.

An essential part of the housekeeping for any service of worship is picking up afterward. Picking up after the Eucharist includes cleansing all the things that have been used and putting them away, straightening the furniture, restoring order to sanctuary, chancel and sacristy. Care in attending to these tasks lightens the responsibilities of workers who are assigned to prepare for subsequent services.

CHAPTER 3

Decorating the Place

$\mathcal{M}$ ost parish altar guilds today are in the position of using, replenishing, or replacing already existing supplies of ornaments, hangings, and other furnishings rather than starting fresh. Perched between yesterday and tomorrow psychologically as well as practically, they are constantly weighing their old customs against the church's (and the world's) new ones and making decisions about suitable ways to decorate for worship. Whether indoors or out, in the church building or in another place, the choices about how to decorate worship space no longer hinge upon what has been done or what must be done to make the place beautiful. Instead they hinge upon what can be done in a particular place, what is artistically appropriate, to make it "a sanctuary where the Lord may dwell."

Over the years certain furnishings have become familiar to worshipers: **altars**, **pulpit** and **lectern**, a **font**, a **litany desk**, **sedilia** (chairs for participants), perhaps a **stoup** for holy water, and **crosses** of several types. There are also books: **Altar Book** (**Missal**, with stand or pillow), **Gospel** and **Lection books**, perhaps a **Lectern Bible**; **alms basins**; and sometimes **icons**, **paintings**, or sculptured or carved **artwork**. And each parish inevitably has its own treasures such as needlepoint kneelers or a Christmas crèche. All these, together with hangings of various kinds, candles, and flowers, enhance worship space.

And all these are in the custody of altar guilds, which are responsible for their care and timely appearance. Because styles change and customs shift and art is constantly being redefined, these ornaments and furnishings, today as always, have contemporary as well as traditional forms. Descriptions in the following sections show the wealth of choices facing an altar guild as it sets out to decorate a place for worship. Several other books are available as well for further reading about the history of church furnishings, hangings, and lights.[8]

HANGINGS IN GENERAL

In the beginning Christians used a wooden table for an altar, first in the home of one of them and later in a house set aside for their worship together. Square, rectangular, round—whatever shape the table, pictures show it draped with a silk, damask, or brocade cloth hanging to the floor. After their later years of secret holy meals around the tombs of martyrs in the catacombs, they began to make tomb-shaped altars for their churches and draped them in a similar way with heavy cloth reminiscent of a funeral pall.

Square altar   *Tomb shape altar*

In either case, the altar represented Christ in the midst of his people, Christ at the table, Christ risen from the tomb, and the altar was treated accordingly. It was the center of worship.

For centuries only the draped cloth was on the table except at the Eucharist, when a clean white cloth was spread on top, and bread, wine, a cup, and eventually a Gospel book were placed on the white cloth. In time Christians adorned the altar cover with bands of material called orphreys and embroidered it with symbols, sometimes jewels, and it became quite elegant. Colors were strong, typically red, in order to draw attention to the center of worship.

The altar was lengthened in the Middle Ages and pushed against the wall so the draped "pall" could no longer be used. A frontal and frontlet were created to take its place. These hangings covered only the visible side of the altar, frontal with frontlet on top. They also were made of rich materials and soon became elaborate with orphreys, fringe, braid, jewels, and embroidered emblems.

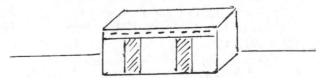

Altar against wall with frontal and frontlet

The familiar hangings of the twentieth century early and late are descendants of these two ancient altar covers. Frontals of all types, frontlets, and altar stoles, fashioned from richly colored tapestries or brocades or from substantial contemporary fabrics, make today's altars wherever they are as visibly central as they are meant to be. It is possible, of course, to omit altar hangings. They aren't required, and omission, too, can effectively focus attention on an altar by letting the beauty of wood or stone—plain or worked by artisans—speak for itself.

When new frontals or hangings for pulpit and lectern are desired, it is important to remember that anyone with a talent for sewing may make them, by hand or by machine. They do not have to be professionally or commercially made. Today throughout the church local artists and craftspeople are urged to use their own talents to decorate their worship spaces. Wonderfully appropriate hangings and other appointments now appear in churches, the product of all sorts of skills in stitchery, even spinning and weaving.

Where parishes find it preferable to go beyond local talent in seeking new hangings, all may be purchased from church supply houses ready-made, made to order, or pre-cut in kits for local needleworkers to finish. They also may be purchased from groups such as religious orders that specialize in making church furnishings. Catalogs provide an excellent guide to what is available.

All hangings may be made of any material suited to the purpose. They do not have to be made of "traditional church fabric" or in a seasonal color or a standard shape. Ideally texture, type, design, color, and ornamentation are chosen to please the artistic sense of the worshipers and to blend with the architecture and existing decor of the building where they will hang. If they are pleasing to the eye, they will provide background for worship, drawing attention to the altar but not dominating it.

Contemporary hangings are alive, in keeping with the idea of celebration. They are made of modern fabrics in a wide range of colors (not necessarily "seasonal") and are basically simple. Decoration is also simple and straightforward. Traditional hangings still have intricate stitchery and ornate design, gold braid and fringe, on rich dark (usually "seasonal") colors of silk and brocade. These hangings blend into the decor of churches that have a feel of antiquity.

The following paragraphs describe the common hangings that can be used for decorating a church, although not one of them has to be. Many contemporary church buildings are so beautiful in themselves that some hangings or all of them seem to be superfluous, and a local decision to omit them entirely is quite appropriate.

Jacobean or Laudean Frontal

Jacobean or *Laudean* is the name that was given to full pall-like altar throws when they were revived in the Church of England in the seventeenth century. This form of drape traces its ancestry to the silk cloth thrown over the earliest wooden tables and then later to the heavy cloth or carpet used to cover stone altars in the manner of a pall. The names are really interchangeable. A Jacobean frontal totally covers a free-standing altar or hangs from three sides of an altar against the wall. It is intended to touch the floor all around, hanging gracefully from the corners. In an attempt to control the fullness around the base of the altar, some have been made with corners loosely or closely fitted. The three-sided version is suspended from a piece of heavy material, dark or light colored, the size of the *mensa* (altar top) and is held in place by a metal bar encased in the hem or by some other mechanism.

Although these full frontals may be made of light-weight material and easily changed, they usually are more substantial (like their ancestors) and their richness and size make them expensive and difficult to store. As a result, they tend to be multicolored or of a color that harmonizes with the decor of the church where they hang in order to be suitable for any season, any occasion. Some churches, nevertheless, have more than one to allow for occasional change— a neutral one for Lent, for example, an elegant one for festivals, and a multicolored one for the rest of the year.

Frontal, Frontlet

A **frontal** hangs to the floor on the long front side of a fixed altar. A **frontlet** (inaccurately called a *superfrontal*) when used, is about five to ten inches deep and hangs over the top edge of the frontal. It may match the frontal or not and may be attached to the frontal instead of hanging over it separately. It may also be used in place of the frontal. Both frontal and frontlet are usually hooked to the front of the altar or suspended from a piece of heavy white or off-white material, originally coarse linen, cut the size of the *mensa* (altar top) and kept in place in a way determined by the altar construction (hooks or a heavy metal bar encased in the linen hem, for example). Frontals require substantial material that drapes well, traditional or contemporary. They may be a single color (not necessarily "seasonal") or neutral or multicolored and may be decorated elaborately or simply with emblems, fringe, braid, or *orphreys* (wide strips of other material appliquéd or otherwise attached). The point of embellishing the frontal is to attract attention to the altar but not distract.

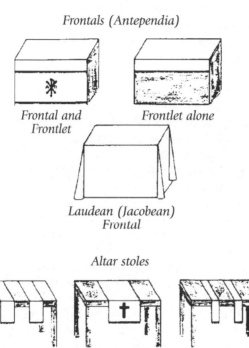

Frontals (Antependia)

Frontal and Frontlet

Frontlet alone

Laudean (Jacobean) Frontal

Altar stoles

Altar Stoles

An altar **stole** (sometimes also called a **frontlet** because it is smaller than a frontal) is a strip of material, narrow or wide, that serves as a frontal. A wide stole is usually used alone; narrow stoles in pairs. Stoles hang from the front of the altar for about three-fourths of the distance to the floor or lie across the altar, hanging both front and back. Altar stoles, like frontals, may be any color and may be fringed or otherwise decorated.

27

Silk Burse and Chalice Veil

In old altar guild manuals the **burse** and **chalice veil** are sometimes listed with vestments (although they vest the chalice, not the clergy), sometimes with hangings because they drape the chalice as hangings drape other furnishings of worship. For many years they have been a familiar sight covering the chalice on the altar, "vesting" it, before and after the Eucharist. Today they are less familiar. Often the altar is now kept bare or at most covered only by the cloths until the Offertory and then cleared entirely after the Communions. This practice has removed the need for "burse and veil." There is no longer a chalice on the altar to vest.

A **burse** (or *corporas case*, as it was once called) is a large cloth-covered stiffened envelope, eight or ten inches square, plain or decorated. It may match the altar hangings and/or the priest's vestments, but it has not always done so nor does it have to. The burse was originally designed to carry two corporals to the table—one to go under the chalice, one to go over it to protect the wine. (The second corporal developed into the stiff pall). The extra purificators now commonly placed in this corporal case have been added through the years for the priest's convenience.

Although the burse is an ancient vestment, the silk **veil** arrived late in the Church of England from Rome and at the time stirred much controversy about its validity as a vestment.[9] A veil is a square of silk or other material, usually but not always matching the burse in design and color. It is often lined for reinforcement so that it will drape well. When a veil is used to vest the chalice, it covers the chalice and paten (plate) on the altar before the Offertory and after the Ablutions. It is large enough to hang to the table on all four sides. The stiff pall placed on the paten gives the veil its "boxed" look.

Until the middle of this century only the priest spread the corporal under the chalice, so the burse containing it was placed on top of the veil. The now common practice of having someone spread the corporal before the service, whether the chalice is on the altar vested or on the *credence* (side table) unvested, has eliminated the original need for the burse, the "corporal case," as a chalice vestment. As a carrying case for extra linens it may quite properly be in some other convenient location.

Pulpit or Lectern Fall

A **pulpit** or **lectern fall** is similar in appearance to an altar stole.

Use is optional, as are color and size. If a fall is used, it hangs from the front of pulpit or lectern, attached by hooks to the lectern or pulpit desk or suspended from a piece of cloth that is thus attached. In the construction and reconstruction of many churches today, pulpit and lectern may be combined, presenting an altar guild a new challenge for decorating when decorating seems called for.

Bible and Missal Markers

Bible and Missal **markers**, once useful, are today primarily decorative and appear less and less frequently. They are made to match the rest of the hangings. If Bible markers are still actually used to mark a lectern Bible, they hang from either the top or the bottom of the Bible, whichever is convenient for the reader. If they are strictly decorative, as is most often the case, they are placed under the open Bible, one to a side, and hang from the top edge secured in place by the weight of the Bible. Because service books today generally come bound with their own ribbon markers, Missal markers have become superfluous. If they are part of a set, they may of course be used either practically or decoratively.

Banners

Banners are suitable for any church building. They may be permanent or seasonal and may hang anywhere in the chancel or nave. They don't usually hang in the sanctuary because they distract attention from the altar. Banners are a teaching device for both young people and adults (as stained-glass windows used to be), so they are suitable throughout the church year, even for penitential seasons. Banners do not have to be "professional" in appearance; in many churches at least some of the year's banners are created by church school children and hang in church as their gift to decorate "God's house."

Dossal and Riddels

A **dossal** is a permanent decorative curtain hung in some manner behind an altar as a backdrop. Although usually a dossal is placed in front of a blank wall to draw attention to the altar space, it can also serve as a screen for an unattractive window or reredos. A dossal is a full drape, simple or ornate. It is usually of heavy material and rich color chosen to blend with whatever other hangings come and go. In the days when altars were against the wall, a

29

dossal could hang from a frame attached to the back of the altar, but in these days of free-standing altars, a dossal hangs from the wall or on a frame against the wall. **Riddels** are tall side curtains that hang from swinging bars attached to the ends of the altar or to the wall behind it. Together with the dossal they make a kind of alcove for the altar. Riddels are no longer common, but if they are used, it is fitting that they blend with the dossal in material and design.

Funeral Pall

A **funeral pall** is a hanging, a vestment, for a casket. *All* caskets in a parish are vested with the same pall (or with an American flag for a member of the armed forces) because all people in the parish are equal in God's sight. A pall can be made by hand or by machine from any material, in any color, with any design, simple or elaborate. It is large enough to cover the casket completely and beautiful enough to preclude any desire to decorate the casket with flowers because *flowers are not placed on caskets in the Episcopal Church*. At one time palls were black, later purple or red, sometimes gold, usually white for children (sized to fit a child's casket). Today palls are usually white in keeping with the fact that "The liturgy for the dead is an Easter liturgy. It finds all its meaning in the resurrection... [and] is characterized by joy" (*BCP*, p. 507).

To vest a container of ashes, either urn or box, a white silk chalice veil is appropriate or a square or circle of white cloth of similar size made just for the purpose. A corporal or a post-communion veil will do. Coverings for urns are available from church supply houses, but they are simple to make if having a veil for this special purpose is desirable. The increase of columbaria and memorial gardens and the direct burial of ashes in the ground "ashes to ashes, dust to dust," have called for new ways to treat the earthly remains of loved ones appropriately. One parish's convenient solution is a small square casket, hand crafted of wood, designed to serve as a temporary container for one person's ashes during a funeral. This type of casket for the parish to share carries the same significance as a funeral pall: all people in the parish are equal in the sight of God.

The Lenten Array

The **Lenten array** is an assortment of unbleached linen, muslin, homespun, or other rough cloth cut in sizes to cover all church furnishings during Lent. The priest's vestments (and the chalice vestments if they are used) usually match. The pieces may be banded in dark red or otherwise simply decorated with dark red symbols of the Crucifixion. Altar, pulpit, lectern, pictures, icons, statues, cross-es—all may be covered. In some churches crosses are covered with just the red; the other furnishings, with the array. (Any decisions about which furnishings to drape and with what are the priest's, not the altar guild's!)

The use of the Lenten array is not new in the Anglican tradition; it is new only to people who are not familiar with it. The Lenten array was customary in the medieval English church but, together with most other vesture and ornaments, fell into disuse early in the reign of Edward VI. Late in the nineteenth century, Percy Dearmer restored most of these things and wrote about them in *The Parson's Handbook*. In the Episcopal Church the Lenten array has gradually come into use during the last quarter of this century, and the custom today is fairly widespread. Its simplicity is in keeping with Lenten discipline.

Parishes that do not use the Lenten array follow the earlier cus-tom of using violet hangings throughout Lent and veiling just the crosses, pictures, and icons in the church at least during Holy Week. Two customs for veil colors are commonly practiced. One uses pur-ple veils from Palm Sunday to Maundy Thursday morning, white for the Maundy Thursday liturgy, and black for Good Friday. The other uses dark red (oxblood) veils for Palm Sunday and all of Holy Week. Either custom is appropriate, but red follows the church calendar.

CANDLES IN GENERAL

Torches, lamps, and candles were incorporated into Christian worship as long ago as the fourth century. Torches were carried before a bishop in procession as a mark of dignity just as they were carried before civil magistrates in Rome. Lamps and candles were hung over the altar or placed around it—sometimes for light, some-times for festivity. But with few exceptions, no candles were placed *on* the altar in the West or in the East until late in the twelfth century. Once the custom began, however, it spread throughout the Christian world. The number of candles on altars multiplied and varied from place to place and era to era. Records of English churches in the Middle Ages show nearly every number of candles up to twenty. But in the sixteenth century an injunction of Edward VI and several other rulings led to the custom of the two altar candles familiar (but hardly universal) in the Church of England and the Episcopal Church today.

In the first years of the Episcopal Church, candles and other ornaments were not common, possibly because of the general feeling about religious simplicity and the subsistence economy of the colonies. But by the late nineteenth century, ornament use had started to grow, and since then there has been little question about placing candles (or crosses or flowers) on the table. Once used principally for illumination, candles are used today because they have come to symbolize Christ the Light of the World and because they are a sign of joy and festivity. In order to be symbolic and festive, however, candles have to be burning. The symbol is in the flame, not the wick, and the festivity in the dancing fire. Unlighted candles serve no more purpose in candle holders than they do in boxes, so it is appropriate in church as at home that they be out of sight unless they are to be lighted. The inclusion of candles in decoration involves the intention to light them.

Although candles at the altar are an expectation of worshipers today, altar candles are not required. Rubrics for the Easter Vigil (*BCP*, p. 294) and the Order for Evening Worship (p. 143) *assume* that candles "at the Altar" are waiting to be lighted. But nowhere in the Prayer Book do the rubrics call for altar candles. In fact, except in those two candlelighting services, in the service for the Dedication of a Church (pp. 574, 576), and in references to the Paschal candle at burial and Baptism (pp. 467, 313) and to a baptismal candle (p. 313), the rubrics never mention candles. People who decorate churches place candles according to customs of the church and the parish and their own artistic sense and good judgment. New ideas can come from observing candle usage in other churches (not just in Episcopal churches!) as well as from pictures and from books about contemporary conduct of worship.

The choice of candles to use in a particular parish depends on the occasion, the traditions of the parish, the equipment on hand, the available space, and other similar variables not the least of which is the money to buy them. Whether wax or oil, candles are expensive. Size, material, shape, and color have to be considered. Any number of any type in any color in any kind of holder may be used for any service as long as the priest responsible for the service approves and the candles will enhance the liturgy, not attract attention to themselves.

The earliest candle material was 100 percent beeswax, which was, of course, pure—hence its significance for use. Eventually, candlemakers learned that reducing the percentage of beeswax with additives would make candles harder, more manageable, and would prolong their life. So wax candles for churches today are generally 51 percent to 100 percent beeswax. Although not beeswax, ordinary stearine candles are satisfactory if an altar guild prefers to use them. Most church candles are white.

Today oil or liquid wax candles are available in all sizes from most church supply houses. They are a convenient substitute for hard wax candles because they don't burn down or drip or drop soot on linens or droop in hot weather. These qualities have convinced many altar guilds to make the change. Oil candles are candle-shaped cylinders. One type holds liquid wax; another type holds cannisters of pure olive oil. Vendors can adapt existing candle holders to fit these cylinders, and the instructions for using and maintaining the candles are not difficult.

Most established church supply houses understand the subject of church candles better than general candle suppliers. Their catalogs are informative and amply illustrated. Both wax candles and oil candle cylinders are ordered by diameter and length instead of purpose, because all churches don't use one size for the same purpose. It is important to consider the appearance of any candles in the place where they are to be used. Although thin candles are graceful, tall thick candles appear sturdier from a distance. Thick wax candles will also burn longer than thin ones, especially if hardened with age.

Finding a way to dispose of wax candle stubs is good church housekeeping. Some altar guilds melt them down to form new candles of all types. Some religious orders accept candle stubs (as a gift) for the same purpose, and some candle suppliers buy back their own candle refuse. In many areas it is possible to find other good uses for them, but disposal is a better economy than accumulation.

Candle holders come in all shapes, sizes, and materials. Church decorators need not be bound by traditional types stored in sacristies or pictured in cataloges. The holder that suits the place where the candle is needed and blends into the background is the one to use on a given occasion. This one could be the church's ornate brass candlestick or it could be a glass candlestick purchased at a rummage sale or borrowed from a parishioner. If it looks "right," it is right. Gold, silver, brass, iron, bronze, aluminum, pewter, plate, pottery, plastic, wood, or stone; tall, short, thin, chunky, simple, ornate, single or multiple: the choice is wide. Candleholders are utilitarian. Mixing types is permissible because the number of candles desired for a purpose determines the number of holders needed, not the number of matching holders at hand in a sacristy. The guiding principle for decorating with candles is good taste.

Candles that are traditional for one parish may not be for another. In the following section are descriptions of the types of candles that the church today has inherited. The list is intended to show the variety of choices and purposes, not to suggest "required" use. New occasions in liturgy may very well call for new candles, and as changes in ceremonial occur, some of these inherited ones may be put aside and new ones introduced. A continuing pattern in the history of candles!

CANDLES IN PARTICULAR

Single candles and **processional torches** explain themselves. They descend from the earliest days of the church, when they were used as much for illumination as for honor. Today they may be used in any multiple anywhere in the church according to the priest's wishes and parish tradition.

Eucharistic candles is a term commonly but inaccurately used for the two or more candles commonly seen on an altar. **Altar candles** is a more accurate term because *eucharistic candles are candles for the Eucharist only.* Altar candles may be used as eucharistic candles, but so may **pavement candles** beside the altar, or **torches** held by acolytes at both ends of whatever serves as the table for the Lord's Supper.

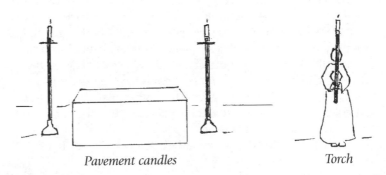

Pavement candles   *Torch*

On the other hand, the two familiar candles on the altar, the **altar candles**, may be lighted for any services conducted from the sanctuary such as weddings or funerals held without the Eucharist. **Eucharistic candles** may be lighted before the Eucharist commences and extinguished at its close, or they may be lighted at the time of the Offertory and extinguished after the Communions. They may even be put in place at the time of the Offertory and removed from the sanctuary after the Communions, as torches and pavement candles are when used as lights for the Eucharist.

Altar candles and eucharistic candles may be tall or short, slender or wide, and they may be wax or oil. For various reasons they usually are white.

No rule governs the number of candles on an altar. For years two candles were traditional, and in earlier times legends grew around the significance of those two. Legends, however, are just that: legends. And after all, as has been noted, the use of any candles on altars in the Episcopal Church has been primarily a development of the twentieth century! If another number than two seems appropriate for a particular altar or a particular occasion or a particular table setting, the altar guild is free to break with tradition. Common sense and artistic good taste guide such a decision.

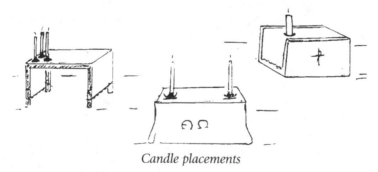

Candle placements

Office lights are candles placed behind or beside an altar with the intention of lighting them for the Office—daily morning or Evening Prayer. It is not required that these candles be lighted for the Office, and they may, in fact, be lighted for any service at all. So the placement, not the use, gives them their name today. Single candles alone or in groups, candelabra of any size, or pavement lights may serve the purpose.

Pavement lights are single tall candles that usually stand on the floor of the sanctuary (the "pavement") although they may stand anywhere in the chancel. They commonly come in two parts: a candlestick with candle and a stand. The candles are white. They are probably descendents of the two candles carried in procession in the early church and then used for reading lights at lectern and altar. Processional torches may double as pavement lights. Carrying the Gospel Book in procession today, to be read in the midst of the people flanked by acolytes carrying torches, is an echo of that early procession.

Candelabra are branched candlesticks usually designed to hold three, five, or seven candles. They may be styled to stand on a table or shelf or on the floor and may be used singly or in any multiple, not necessarily "balanced." They are white.

The **bishop's candle** is an extra single candle placed on the altar or the retable when the bishop of a diocese visits a parish and presides at the Eucharist. The candle is unobtrusive; its significance lies in its presence as an extra light. The custom of using a bishop's candle is by no means common, but a number of parishes have adopted it.

The **Paschal candle** has the special purpose of being lighted from the fire newly kindled at the Great Vigil of Easter (*BCP*, p. 285), then carried in procession to the chancel and placed in its stand to burn (p. 287) during every service in the church from Easter to Pentecost. The Paschal candle stands at the font during the rest of the year where it is lighted for Baptisms and is the source of light for baptismal candles (p. 313). It may be carried at the head of funeral processions (p. 467) and is sometimes used as a "Christ candle" in the center of an Advent wreath.

Paschal candles may be wax or oil and may be purchased or handmade. They are as a rule tall and wide, but some are extraordinarily so, some short, and some thin. A Paschal candle is, of course, white, as it is the Easter candle. But it may be decorated for Eastertide in any way, simply or elegantly, as may its holder.

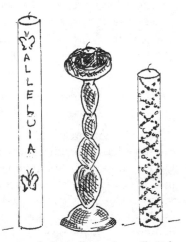

Paschal candles and candlestick

An **Advent wreath** is a circular candle holder for four or five candles—four for the four Sundays in Advent with an optional "Christ candle" in the center for Christmas Eve. This Christ candle is white; the other four may be white, blue, purple, or a combination of three purple and one pink for Gaudete Sunday, the third Sunday in Advent. The candles mark the progress of worshipers through the four weeks of Advent, one more being lighted each Sunday in succession around the wreath until all four (or five with the Christ candle) are burning on Christmas Eve. The wreath may be made of any material, but lighted candles require a sturdy base, so metal or wood are most satisfactory. The wreath may be suspended from the ceiling or placed on some kind of stand in full view of the worshipers. Advent wreaths are frequently decorated with greens, preferably broad-leafed evergreens so they will last the four weeks. Flowers aren't appropriate because Advent is a penitential season, but cones or pods or berries may be added to the greens. The decorative materials must be treated to resist fire.

A **sanctuary light** is a candle encased in glass for long-term burning, usually a week. Shape, size, and term of burning vary, however. Originally, sanctuary lights were the several lamps hung across the sanctuary to light the altar. In time they came to signify God's presence in the church building. From this significance grew the practice of burning a candle night and day in front of a *tabernacle* (a locked box on or above the altar) or an *aumbry* (a wall safe, usually in or just outside the sanctuary) in which the Sacrament is reserved.

Baptismal candles are usually ten to twelve inches long and sized to fit normal home candle holders. A baptismal candle is lighted from the Paschal candle at a Baptism and presented to the newly baptized person (*BCP*, p. 313). This custom is hardly new; it was introduced in the fourth century.[10] Any white candle is appropriate, but those available from church supply houses are generally decorated to suit the occasion.

Miscellaneous candles may be needed from time to time for liturgical use or decoration. The occasion usually determines the size and color and number required, and any candle shop will probably fill the need.

Several **candle accessories** are familiar to altar guilds. They are designed to increase the efficiency of candle use. **Followers** (glass, brass, or chrome cylinders made to fit over wax candle tops) prevent drips, prolong candle life, and keep flames even. They can be ordered from church supply houses by candle diameter. To keep followers free from wax buildup, rinse them regularly with very hot water and wipe them with paper towels. *When removing wax with water in a sink* protect the drain by adding tri-sodium phosphate (TSP) to the rinse water or using a separate basin to be emptied elsewhere. TSP breaks up the wax. **Bobeches** are glass or plastic collars for candles or candle sockets to catch drips. (Singular or plural, the word has only two syllables, the second one accented.) Clean bobeches as above, with hot water, TSP, and paper towels. Both **Candle tubes** and **candle joiners** extend the life of candles. White, off-white, or colored **tubes** hold stubs or broken, misshapen, or mismatched candles on a spring base that feeds them to the top and allows them to burn to the last flicker. **Joiners** are couplers, usually metal, that hold two candle stubs, thereby allowing the top candle to burn an extra few inches. Tubes and couplers are still available at some church supply houses.

A **candle taper/extinguisher** is a useful accessory. Most churches have more than one, usually brass, in different lengths. Keeping the bell top of an extinguisher clean is important because soot accumulates in it even when it is used only with oil candles. Soot, if it drops, stains whatever it touches. Taper wicks need to be trimmed regularly (as do candle wicks) so they, too, won't shed soot particles and so they will burn efficiently. Wicks in oil candles do not require trimming.

FLOWERS

Flowers at the table are a gift to the glory of God. They aren't necessary in church, but when they appear they provide a finishing touch to an already beautiful scene. Flowers speak of life and festivity. In fact, the only rubric in the entire Prayer Book that even mentions them refers to a festive occasion—the Dedication and Consecration of a Church (p. 576). In that service, "as the furnishings of the church are dedicated, they may be decorated by members of the congregation with flowers..." The altar is included by implication because the altar will be dedicated. For hundreds of years flowers decked churches for festivals, but not until late in the nineteenth century did flowers become acceptable decorations on the table in either the Church of England or the Episcopal Church.[11] And even then they weren't required. Worshipers in those days didn't think of flowers being "normal" altar decoration. But today they do, and on special occasions they expect flowers elsewhere in the church as well. In fact, people are so accustomed to seeing flowers in church and on the altar that they are quite likely to question their absence except during Advent or Lent, when it is common to see bare altars or altars decorated at the most with plain greens or dry branches and berries.

Flower arranging for an altar is not a competition; flower show standards of form, distribution, and content don't apply. Arrangers of altar flowers have no reason to feel restricted by the expectations of others or burdened by the numerous ideas expressed about "proper" arrangements. with a minimum of practice *anyone* can arrange flowers for an altar. Learning comes from doing it and from accepting one's own effort. In this effort, more than most, one is one's own worst critic! Some basic knowledge about plants and their characteristics, some common sense, and a feeling about overall effective decoration—the beauty of the whole instead of the parts—will guide most people through creating presentable flower arrangements. Certainly some people are quicker at learning and more adept at doing than others, but anyone can make an acceptable offering.

Basic knowledge about flowers can be acquired from books on flowers and flower arranging (fresh and dried), books that are practical rather than arty or professional.[12] The common sense about arranging comes from experience. The feeling about effective decoration comes from observation. The only standard for church arrangements is that flowers at the altar or in any other area blend into the background rather than draw attention to themselves. They are there to increase the beauty of the place, not to please the congregation.

What is "appropriate" is whatever natural materials can be made attractive at a given time for a given situation. Any flowers are appropriate: garden, greenhouse, field, or forest, even the blossoms that people call weeds. The rest of God's creation is also appropriate: leaves and branches, greens and grasses, nuts and berries, vegetables and fruits, pods and tassels. Breads, dried flowers, potted plants, sea shells, trees, and stones are appropriate if they work well in an arrangement. All of these speak of life in one way or another. On the altar they are a gift to God representing life on earth.

In the past it has not been the practice to use even the most exquisite artificial flowers for the altar. Altar flower people frequently ask why. The old reason that "they are only a copy of life and aren't truly a gift of God" pales before the argument that the imagination and artistry behind artifical flowers *are* truly gifts of God, even if the flowers are produced commercially. In some churches, for one reason or another, those flowers are the only solution to decorating an altar. So expediency has affected practice in this area, too, and lovely arrangements of delicate artificial flowers have in many places beautified altars that would otherwise have had to do without.

Any container for flowers is appropriate if it holds the flowers of the day well and if it is clean. A container may be an ancient brass vase from the sacristy closet or any other receptacle from any source—even a kitchen cupboard. As long as a container has a useful shape and will hold water, it will do.[13] An arrangement of any design is appropriate if it fits the space nicely. Any color is appropriate for any season. Any number of blossoms is appropriate. Symmetry is appropriate, but asymmetry is also appropriate if effective. One arrangement on the altar or near it, or two, or three— whatever truly beautifies the space is appropriate.

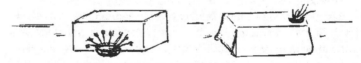

Flower Placement

In many parishes altar flower committees gather their own floral materials from the world around them or from church cutting gardens. Consequently, they never face a problem of insufficient funds to buy flowers. In other parishes, where flowers are purchased Sunday by Sunday and dependent on week by week contributions, altar flower arrangers have to seek income to meet expense. If through the years contributions for flowers have become tied to prayers for certain Sundays, the difficulty in working out a predictable flower budget is increased. Some parishes have set up revolving flower funds (separate from prayer requests) to which contributions may be made at any time and from which flowers are purchased all the time.

The whole purpose of flowers in church is to add beauty— not to dominate, not to distract, not to disrupt the worship that is taking place. For that reason, *in the Episcopal Church it is customary to discourage a profusion of flowers at the front of the church.* The goal is to limit flowers in the sanctuary to two or three arrangements on or near the altar. This practice often leads to difficult situations at weddings or funerals or other special services (even at Christmas and Easter) when many flowers are desired or given and sometimes arrive at the church unexpectedly. Extra flowers at these times may be placed in other areas of the church where they will add beauty but not be center stage. Questions may be asked about this custom, and those who prepare the church for the services can often be very helpful to the priest by explaining the reasons for it.

In some parishes those who do the rest of the decoration manage all the steps of floral decoration. In other parishes a flower committee is in charge. A flower committee needs guidance by the priest and the altar guild leader in order to understand the purpose of flowers in the church and the possibilities open to it in placing them there. As a rule, professional flower people (such as florists, decorators, and bridal consultants) are not invited to help because they usually do not have liturgical understanding about what they are doing.

As long as the people working with flowers have the priest's blessing, they are free to try almost any floral decoration at the altar and around the church from indoor gardens of spring flowers at Easter representing the garden at the tomb to the "holly and ivy, box and bay, put in the church on Christmas Day" symbolizing the new life and joy brought by the Christ Child. Each church lends itself to imaginative ideas for decorating with flowers. Arrangements at the altar are hardly the limit of what can be done to make the building come alive. Finding unexpected places to add touches of beauty with flowers is a continuing challenge.

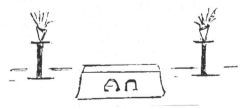

Flower Placement

CHAPTER 4

Setting the Table

*O*nce the worship place is clean and decorated with appropriate hangings, flowers, and candles, and the alms basins and books for the service are in place, it is time to focus on the table and the dishes and linens and food for the celebration.

HISTORY

In the first years of the church, Christian Jews continued their pattern of going to the synagogue on the Sabbath for Scripture reading, Psalms, and teaching. But when other Jews went home for prayers and the Sabbath meal, the Christians went to the home of one of the group for teaching about Christ, intercessory prayer in his name, and the Kiss of Peace, and for their meal together where they shared bread and wine as he had commanded. In this way they started the Eucharist. As the number of Christians increased and groups formed in different places, it became usual for them to adapt one large home to accommodate Christians of an area and to gather there for a combined Jewish-Christian Liturgy of the Word, followed by the Christian meal. They began to gather on Sunday instead of the Sabbath and to limit the meal to breaking the Bread and sharing the Cup because the group was large. Ceremonial grew as the rite grew and the Word spread. But the core of the Eucharist stayed firm.

When Christianity became legal in the fourth century and Christians were free to meet in public buildings, they continued to worship according to the pattern developed in those early years. First everyone, baptized and unbaptized alike, gathered in a large room around a pulpit or an *ambo* (a podium) for the Word (Scripture readings both old and new, the Psalms, and teaching). Then the unbaptized people were dismissed. The baptized joined in the intercessory prayers, followed by the Kiss of Peace and, in another part of the room (or a smaller room), the Liturgy of the

43

Table. The table in the beginning had been just a square wood table in someone's home; so was this one just a square wood table, but a table reserved for a special purpose. Deacons covered it with a white cloth, and worshipers presented bread and wine to them for the meal. They placed these gifts on the table so that all could "make Eucharist" together.[14]

In succeeding years the square table was elongated and eventually made of stone. Candles, linens, and vessels of silver, gold, and other rich materials were placed on it in abundance. The importance of these adornments soon overshadowed the importance of the table itself. They began to acquire allegorical meanings and imagined characteristics.

In the Middle Ages the room of the table became what is now the sanctuary, the holy place, separated from the teaching area by a rood screen (an openwork partition containing a cross). Furnishings continued to multiply. During the years of the Reformation and its aftermath, both in England and later in America, much of the ornamentation of the table (and the room and the clergy) was removed. But bit by bit it returned. It continued to return well into the twentieth century. Part of the liturgical renewal of this last fifty years has been a leap backward to the early days of the church, to that time before the Middle Ages when the table was bare until the gifts were presented and then was set with simplicity.

It is no more necessary for altars always to be set in the same way than it is necessary for churches to be decorated in the same way or the participants dressed in the same way or the worship to follow a single pattern. *The Book of Common Prayer* is inclusive. It doesn't intend one way to be the only way in the church or in one parish as long as the Eucharist remains "the principal act of Christian worship on the Lord's Day and other major Feasts" (p. 13). Instruction for that occasion is basic: "The Holy Table is spread with a clean white cloth during the celebration" (p. 406); bread and wine are returned to God from the congregation at the Offertory (pp. 333, 361), placed on the table by the deacon (or an appropriate minister) with one cup for the wine "and, if need be, a flagon" (pp. 322, 354, 407). Then with the words our Lord used at the Last Supper as recorded in the Gospel, the bread and wine are offered by the priest to be blessed, broken, and given back as the Body and Blood of Christ. These few rubrics for the Eucharist allow great latitude to those who plan for it.

Today those who plan parish liturgy have gained new insight about variety in worship and are becoming creative about it. Although priests make the final decisions, they may involve as many of the congregation in planning services as seems practical— the altar guild and a liturgical committee, for example. The guidelines are brief: the rubrics, the bishop's wishes, and parish traditions. Every parish history is full of traditions! Considering those traditions in planning is pastorally important, but changing them is frequently important, too. Parochial customs may be far from rubrical and can sometimes control a congregation with old practices that stifle freedom in worship. Every parish also has its own personality and its own limitations; considering them is necessary in the planning process. Once the plans are made, however, *the responsibility of altar guild workers everywhere is to devise practical methods for putting the plans into effect with reverence and beauty.* It goes without saying that it is just as impossible to give specific directions for "setting the table"—directions that will apply to all altar guilds in all parishes at all times— as it is to give specific directions for "decorating."

In general, the vessels and linens that are to be used for the Eucharist are expected to be clean and in designated places at a predetermined time, and the bread and wine ready. An agreed upon procedure makes everyone who is involved in preparation comfortable and confident. Part of that procedure is having every task completed well before a service starts. A last minute scurry of altar guild workers disturbs both the atmosphere of a church ready for worship and the meditations of worshipers who arrive early for a time of quiet.

PROCEDURE

Currently, parishes of the Episcopal Church follow two methods of setting the table for the Eucharist. One has the vested chalice on the altar before the service begins; the other has the altar bare until the Offertory. Either method is totally acceptable. The priest in charge decides which to follow when. Some priests follow the first or the second exclusively; other priests alternate the two for various pastoral reasons. In some dioceses the bishop prefers one method; the priest, the other. So the bishop's visitations may provide the only opportunity that parish has to widen its worship experience.

When the table is to be totally bare until the Offertory (as it was in the early church), someone has to spread the fair linen (the "clean white cloth") so the deacon can set the Bread and Cup on it. Someone also has to put the Missal on the altar and place the eucharistic candles on it or next to it and light them. The deacon, the servers or other assistants, altar guild members, or other members of the congregation may do all this at the time of the Offertory. As an alternative, before the service begins altar guild workers may spread the altar cloth (or uncover the cloth already on the altar and change it if necessary); place the Missal; spread the corporal (a small white cloth to go under the chalice); and have the eucharistic candles ready for lighting. "Bare until the Offertory" means that the altar guild places the principal chalice, vested or unvested, on the credence (or on another side table in the sanctuary or in the sacristy) ready for the deacon to transfer to the altar at the Offertory.

For the first method, altar guild workers prepare the table before the service as outlined above—linen, corporal, Missal, candles. And they place the principal chalice on the corporal on the altar, "vested." Vesting the chalice is a practice developed for convenience late in the life of the church and generally followed until recently. For the years while "vesting" was the only practice, diagrams of a vested chalice were often posted on the walls of sacristies to guide altar guilds. Because these are not common today, a copy of that diagram is in Appendix 6. Descriptions of the items used are in the "Vessels" and "Linens" sections of this book.

To vest a chalice, nest the paten in the bowl of the chalice for ease in carrying the two together, placing a purificator (a small white cloth) between the two as a cushion to prevent scratches. If a priest's wafer is to be used, place it either on the paten or in the bread box with the people's wafers. A stiff pall (a small reinforced square of white cloth) placed on the paten serves as a form over which to drape the chalice veil. For years a burse was set on top of all, a stiff fabric envelope holding the corporal that the priest would spread under the chalice. If the corporal is spread before the service, the burse (the former corporal case) no longer carries a corporal, so placing it on the chalice really belies its purpose. Using it to hold small linens and putting it somewhere else is an option.

A **credence table** or shelf is a serving table to hold the vessels and linens that will be used at the altar. If possible, it is at the right of the priest standing at the altar, the side of the deacon, for convenience in serving. In sanctuaries where the altar has been moved away from the east wall to be free standing, and the credence is still fixed to the east or south wall, ceremonial has to be adjusted or a new credence arrangement devised.

Altar guild workers arrange items on the credence to be convenient for the priest and servers, so a mutually agreed upon pattern for the arrangement is important for everyone's peace of mind. A white cloth usually covers the credence for cleanliness. Then whatever will be used for the Liturgy of the Table is placed on it: water in a small bottle, cruet, or pitcher; an extra chalice or two for chalice bearers at the service; possibly small bowls, baskets, or plates for assistants who serve the Bread; perhaps a container of additional wine. If the credence is small, some of these things may be left in the sacristy until called for. If the altar is to be bare, the principal chalice, vested or unvested, may go on the credence, as noted above. Any necessary small linens may be placed there, too, either in a neat pile or in a burse. If the lavabo ceremony is practiced, a lavabo and towel are added.

The bread and the wine of the Offertory are placed on a table in the nave, located where all the people can see their offering. The location depends on the building. It may be near the entrance; it may be in the center aisle or near the chancel steps. A white cloth may cover this table. Some parishes place flowers on it; others place a lighted candle there, extinguished when oblationers take the bread and wine to the altar. In some situations communicants arriving for the service break pieces from the loaf (or take individual wafers from a container) and put them in the bowl or basket used for the presentation. In some parishes the bread and wine are provided each week by different members of the church body who present the gifts themselves at the Offertory on behalf of the whole community.

A loaf of bread may be presented on a towel or a serving dish. The wine may be presented in a cruet, a flagon, a beaker, a pitcher, a decanter, a bottle, or some other like container that is large enough to hold wine for the expected number of communicants. Only one chalice goes on the altar during the Prayer of Consecration (*BCP*, p. 407). It may be necessary to add a flagon, because all the wine for the Eucharist is to be consecrated at the same time. After the Fraction, extra chalices are filled with wine for chalice bearers and small containers with bread for assistant ministers, and bread and wine are also placed in containers for Lay Eucharistic Ministers to carry to hospitalized and homebound members of the parish if that is a parish practice.

Eucharistic candles are extinguished, perhaps removed, after the Communions or at the close of the service. Altar guild workers cover the fair linen with a protector to keep it clean, or they remove it from the altar and put it away. The dishes and the soiled linens are taken to the sacristy after the Communions or the Ablutions (by servers) or the Dismissal (by altar guild workers), then cleansed and stored. Vessels and linens that have been used with the consecrated bread and wine are rinsed before washing, either into a piscina that drains onto the ground or in a bowl of water that is emptied onto the ground.

Priests have different instructions about treating the remnants of the Sacrament. According to the rubric (*BCP*, p.409) "the celebrant or deacon, or other communicants [including altar guild members], reverently eat and drink it, after the Communion of the people or after the Dismissal." In some parishes the priest does the Ablutions at the altar after the Communion and consumes the remnants at that time. In other parishes the table is cleared immediately after the Communions by the deacon or another attendant, and the vessels and remnants (covered with a corporal) are placed on the credence or in the sacristy to be taken care of later as the priest directs. Remnants of consecrated bread and wine are always either reserved or consumed by whomever the priest appoints. (Leavened bread can't be reserved because it won't keep well, and wine keeps for only a short time.)

When the service is finished, the sanctuary and all other worship areas and the sacristy are restored to order. Every item that has been used is put away; flowers are bundled for delivery according to parish custom; furniture is straightened; the floor is swept, if necessary. Altar guild workers leave the church building in order, just as they would like to find it if they were arriving to start their work.

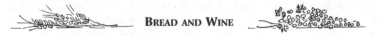

BREAD AND WINE

In the beginning, the Bread of the Christian Eucharist was "real" bread, leavened or unleavened, bread recognizable as bread in texture and taste to the people sharing it. Jewish bread came first, the bread of the regular meal. As the church expanded, Jewish bread was followed by whatever bread was usual to succeeding worshiping groups. This practice continued for eleven hundred years.

Early bread

Wafers first appeared in western Christendom in the Middle Ages during a period of many other shifts and adjustments in customs and ceremonies that were explained with allegories or pietistic reasoning. At first they were large wafers that were broken into pieces for distribution; then they were individual wafers, each placed in the mouth of a communicant instead of the hand. And because of attendant circumstances in Christian liturgical history in the West, wafers, administered in one of these ways, remained the bread of the Eucharist for years.

Real bread has changed places with wafers more than once, however, sometimes by local preference, sometimes by church ruling, sometimes in quick succession. For example, the 1549 English Prayer Book ruled that the "unleavened and rounde" bread (wafers) "bee made through all thys realme...somethyng more larger and thicker than it was, so that it may be aptly deuided in diuers pieces," and the 1552 book countered with "it shall suffyse that the Bread bee such as is usuall to bee eaten... wyth other meates, but the best and purest wheate bread that conueniently may be gotten."[15] In the United States, whatever variety of real bread was broken for the infrequent Eucharists in the Episcopal Church of colonial days, "round wafers" took the place of broken bread in the mid-nineteenth century and became customary for generations. Nuns in Episcopal convents were the church's "wafer makers," although in time church supply houses offered them for sale as well. White, brown, thick, thin, square, round, plain, decorated, purchased, or homemade—all types of wafers have been used.

Wafers

During the last half of the twentieth century the Episcopal Church has gradually been going back to the use of real bread on the table, regularly or at least for special occasions. Sharing a loaf of bread widens the worshipers' understanding of "returning" gifts to God. Often parishioners are asked to make it, altar guilds included. Today loaves of bread of all sizes, shapes, and derivation appear on altars —leavened and unleavened, plain and sweet, white and brown. Once again bread that is usual to the worshiping community is the Bread of the Eucharist, the offering of the whole community, presider and people alike. Once again a single loaf is broken and shared by all.

Contemporary bread

The action of tearing a loaf of bread apart at the Fraction has a powerful visual and spiritual effect on presider and people alike. To quote Louis Weil, "I can say as a priest, when I've been given a large loaf of bread for the Fraction and I have every muscle in my arm working to break the bread apart, I know what the Fraction is at that point. I physically know what the Fraction is!"[16] All the people worshiping see the one loaf, the one Body of Christ, torn apart before their eyes. And then it is given to them, the Body of Christ in that place. A line from Bishop Jeffery Rowthorn sums it up: "Bread doesn't break easily and neatly; instead it tears with difficulty and leaves rough edges for all to see. That is more akin to our experience because we don't let God break us and use us in any neat and easy fashion. Instead there are rough edges that all can see. So whenever you put the bread on the altar, remember that God is intent on breaking us and using us as the gifts of God for the people of God scattered across the face of the earth."[17] In the presence of that image, any problems presented by possible crumbs become insignificant!

Whole pita and torn apart pita

The wine of the Eucharist in the early church was red, the common wine of the people. Although it has been white or golden in some eras since ("sips of white wine" in place of red in nineteenth-century Episcopal use), red wine is found in most churches today—robust red wine. Any wine can be the wine of the table, commercial or homemade, sweet or dry, and the types can vary. One altar guild responsibility is to be sure the supply of wine, as well as bread, is always ample. Even when both are carried to the service by parishioners, a reserve supply is good practice in case of emergency.

Bread and wine have been associated with religious meals and ceremonies, the heart of a people's Being, from as far back as we have knowledge of these things. Although the Christian Eucharist has its direct origin in the Sabbath meal of its Jewish heritage, its roots lie in the earliest practices of human beings at worship. Bread is "the staff of life," which people have made from God's gift of grain. At the Offertory the people present their bread, the symbol of their life, to God who returns it to them consecrated, the symbol of his life in the Body of Christ. And the people present wine that they have made from God's gift of fruit, wine that bubbles with life of its own. They give wine as the symbol of fellowship and joy and fullness of life on earth, and it, too, is consecrated and given back as the bonding, life-giving Blood of Christ.

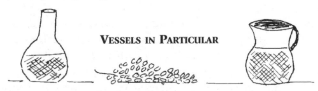

VESSELS IN PARTICULAR

The basic vessel of the church is the common cup of the Eucharist, the chalice. All the other vessels, familiar and unfamiliar, have been added for convenience through the years as the liturgy with its rites and ceremonies has developed. None of these others is essential, but several of them in one form or another help those who conduct church services to do so with ease and dignity. Knowing about each, its purpose and its possible forms, is part of altar guild background. So is knowing that only one cup is essential.

Chalice

A **chalice** or cup holds the wine of the Eucharist, wine mixed with a little water. It is usually about eight to twelve inches tall, footed, with a plain or decorated knob (knop, knurl) on the stem to serve as an aid for holding it firm. Traditionally, a chalice has been silver or gold, sometimes simple, sometimes exquisitely crafted with filigree and jewels. Chalices like this abound in the church and are readily available from artisans and church supply houses. But today other cups in many shapes, sizes, and materials are also available, handcrafted or commercially made. Any other material such as pottery, ceramic, glass, stone, pewter, aluminum, or steel is appropriate, as is any shape or size of cup that is suitable for the group and the occasion and the place. What is required is a cup. What is desirable is a cup or chalice that represents excellence in workmanship and is large enough to be seen by every worshiper when it is on the table. One chalice, one cup, is sufficient as long as there is a container of wine to refill it. Most parishes have at least one extra for a chalice bearer to administer or for an emergency.

Chalices

Paten

Although the rubric implies that the bread is placed directly on the altar, a custom of providing some sort of container for the bread developed in the early days of the church. A *paten* is the long-time plate for the bread, the plate for consecration, the plate for serving. Today a paten is no longer mentioned in the rubrics: the priest holds the bread itself or lays a hand on it to consecrate it. Traditionally, paten and chalice have matched in design because the two have been treated as a "set," the one usually nested in the other before and after the service. They don't have to match, however, nor do they have to be nested even when they do match. Although once it was thought that the bread could rest only on silver or gold, patens today are as varied in material as chalices.

Appropriate patens

When a loaf of bread is the eucharisic bread, it is possible for it to be presented, blessed, broken, and shared without using any kind of plate. However, containers for "real bread" are practical. They are chosen to fit the loaf—a large plate, a platter, a bowl, or a basket, for example. Some parishes have several, to be ready for different occasions or different sizes of loaf. A large container would hold the loaf for the Offertory procession and for the consecration as well. Many parishes have extra bread containers for assistant ministers.

Ciborium, Bread Box

The use of the **ciborium** and the **bread box** depends on local practice. Both containers are designed to hold wafers and will not conveniently hold any other bread. Either may be used in the Offertory procession or to hold the reserved sacrament. A *ciborium* is similar to a chalice but has a cover with something such as a standing cross or a knob on top for a handle. A *bread box* has no standard size, shape, or design. A parish using loaf bread has no need for either vessel except perhaps for reserving consecrated wafers (because leavened bread cannot be successfully reserved). Both vessels have traditionally been silver or gold, often matched to the rest of the silver or gold vessels, but both may be made of any other material suitable for the purpose, such as wood, glass, pewter, or earthenware.

Flagon, Pitcher

The rubric (*BCP*, p. 407) "it is appropriate that there be only one chalice on the Altar" mentions a **flagon** for extra wine from which to fill other chalices following the Prayer of Consecration. A flagon is an oversized cruet holding approximately a quart. Shape, material, and size are a matter of preference. It may hold the wine of the Offertory, but a pitcher, a decanter, a bottle, a carafe, or any other similar container may hold the wine in its place.

Cruets

Two cruets, one for wine and one for water, have been usual for preparing the chalice before the Prayer of Consecration. Size, shape, and material depend on local requirements and preference. Cruets need not match the chalice and paten. They need not even match each other, nor do both have to be side by side. A cruet of water for preparing the chalice (and performing the lavabo and Ablutions ceremonies, if they are practiced) may be on the credence; a cruet of wine for the offering, on a table with the bread in the nave. An average-sized, one-cup cruet is probably big enough for all the required water, but an average-sized cruet may not be big enough for the wine of the offering. In that case, a flagon or some other larger container may take its place on the oblations table in the nave.

Lavabo

A **lavabo** is a small bowl still used in many churches for a ceremonial washing of the priest's fingers before the Great Thanksgiving. When used, the bowl is on the credence table together with a towel. Shape, size, and material depend on local preference. The lavabo ceremony is ancient, originating at the time when priests received all sorts of gifts from the people at the Offertory and really needed to wash their hands before blessing and breaking the bread. Today it is not common for priests to practice this act except after distributing ashes or anointing with holy oil or participating in other ceremonies that make cleansing the fingers necessary.

Pyx

A **pyx** is a box the size of a watch case, usually silver or gold, used by a priest for carrying the consecrated bread to individuals away from the church. A pyx may have a leather or cloth case and an attached cord or chain so it can be worn around the neck.

The Priest's Communion Kit

Many parishes or priests have a set of miniature eucharistic vessels, commonly silver, silver plate, or pewter but often of some other material. A complete kit usually contains a chalice, a paten, a bread box, cruets, a small white cloth, and sometimes a cross, candlesticks, and a spoon (occasionally needed to serve wine)—the essentials for setting a table for a private Communion. Marion Hatchett suggests avoiding "doll-sized" sets when possible, "for they trivialize the sacrament."[18] Slightly larger sets similar to "chaplains' kits" are available.

Today in many parishes Lay Eucharistic Ministers carry the Sacrament in both kinds directly from the altar to sick or homebound parishioners who cannot be present at worship. This practice revives another custom of the early church. People in this ministry have devised their own cases for carrying the bread and wine for their mission safely and with dignity. For example, some fit a pyx or a small cloth envelope holding the bread and a small bottle holding the wine as well as a clean napkin, a small glass, and a spoon into a box or basket or other carrying case just the right size for this purpose.

Oil Stock

A **stock** is a small screw-top cylindrical container for carrying the anointing oils into church or into homes or hospital. Some are designed to be worn as rings, some to be cupped in the hand, some to be placed on any flat surface. Some oil stocks are fashioned with more than one compartment for keeping separate the oils for different purposes.

Holy oils are part of the Judeo-Christian tradition. They were designated for specific uses in Christian ceremonies in early centuries when bishops began to consecrate oils for anointing in Baptism and in healing. The oil for Baptism (olive oil with balsam or another aromatic substance added) is *chrism*. The oil for healing (just olive oil) is *unction*. A third oil, the *oil of catechumens* (also pure olive oil) was used in preparing catechumens for Baptism, and is used in some parishes today. Generally, the holy oils, two and sometimes three, are consecrated by the bishop of a diocese during Holy Week and distributed in vials to priests throughout the diocese for use during that year. At the end of that year the old oil is reverently discarded.[19] The rubrics in the 1979 *Book of Common Prayer* provide for a bishop to consecrate oil for chrism in a parish at the time of Baptism (p. 298) and for a priest to consecrate oil for unction at the time for anointing (p. 455). In the Episcopal Church anointing is optional, perhaps because for three hundred years it was not mentioned in the Prayer Book. Although unction was finally restored in 1928 and chrism in 1979, change—even change back to old customs—takes time.

Baptismal Bowl

If the font does not have a drain direct to the ground, it is customary to use an auxiliary bowl inside the font to hold the water of Baptism, which can then be poured onto the ground or into a sacristy piscina. Lovely footed or Revere-shaped silver bowls are often used for this purpose, but a baptismal bowl may be of any material.

Unless a Baptism away from a font takes place in a natural setting where there is water, a bowl is needed there as well.

Some Episcopal churches keep a similar bowl of water that has been blessed at the entrance to the nave. This holy water is a reminder to each person who enters of the promises of Baptism, and all are invited to dip their fingers into it and "cross themselves" with a silent prayer of rededication. A fixed container for holy water comparable to a font is called a **stoup**, and some Episcopal churches have these. Some have given this new purpose to old fonts no longer in use. But just as candles stand in the sanctuary in anticipation of being lighted, so a stoup stands at the church entrance in anticipation of holding holy water. An altar guild task is to see that it does, that it is kept clean, and that the standing water does not stagnate. An auxiliary bowl in the stoup simplifies the task. A bowl of holy water can be emptied into the piscina or onto the ground when necessary and the bowl washed and replenished.

Shell

A **shell** is a scallop-shaped scoop, usually silver, for spooning baptismal water on the head of the candidate. Use of a shell is a late addition to the ceremonial of Baptism and is entirely optional. The priest's hand is as effective today as it was before shells appeared.

Ewer

A **ewer** is a pitcher. Among church vessels, small ewers sometimes take the place of cruets. But generally a church ewer is a large pitcher used for pouring the water of Baptism into the font or pouring the water for washing feet on Maundy Thursday into a basin. Any large pitcher is suitable.

When a baptismal bowl is used in the font, the need for a ewer has been questioned because the bowl can be filled before it is put in place. Using a ewer, however, or even a smaller pitcher, is liturgically important because pouring the water from it allows everyone present to see and to hear the outward and visible sign of the sacrament.

Thurible (Censer), Boat, and Spoon

The ceremonial use of incense in procession and in worship goes back in Christian liturgy to at least the sixth century. Through the years it has been used with varied significance at different points in the liturgy. Today "the cloud of incense rising heavenward" is basically a symbol of prayer, and the practice is optional in the Episcopal Church. If directions are needed, they can be found in a priest's manual.

The **boat** is the container for the incense which is spooned into the **thurible** and burned over charcoal. Thurible, boat, incense, spoon, charcoal, tongs, and matches are generally stored together for the convenience of the **thurifer** (the censer bearer).

Sanctus Bell

A sanctus bell may be a single bell, a cluster of three or four bells, or a gong. When a sanctus bell is part of the ceremonial, it is placed on the floor at the Epistle end of the altar. During the celebration of the Eucharist, the server customarily rings it at the Sanctus and just before the words "For in the night in which he was betrayed" in any form of the Great Thanksgiving. (In days when elevation of the Host was a ceremonial act, the bell was also rung then.)

The many different styles of all these vessels are amply illustrated in standard church supply house catalogs. These catalogs show for the most part silver, silver plate, gold, and possibly pewter—only a fraction of the materials in use in the church today. Craftsmen and commercial establishments specializing in other materials also publish catalogs. Examining them, too, before purchasing vessels is important in order to discover today's range of choices. Some parishes are blessed with artists capable and desirous of producing some of these vessels in a form to suit the community's needs. With the priest's approval, these also are appropriate and truly an offering from the community to the glory of God.

CARING FOR VESSELS

If the vessels are made of material other than silver or gold, cleaning them is simple. Wash vessels in hot water using a mild soap, rinse well, then dry with a soft dish towel, rubbing briskly to make the vessels shine. Good care includes storing vessels in cloth bags to keep them clean between uses and to prevent scratches, chips, and dents. Store vessels where they won't be easily broken. Silver and gold vessels and gold wash linings are best cared for by the same method— hot water, mild soap, and a soft towel. Storage in bags of Pacific cloth or some other tarnish resistant material is a good idea. According to reputable silversmiths, silver lasts longer if it is not polished frequently. Gold should be polished *only* by a goldsmith or a jeweler.

Vessels set with precious or semiprecious stones require special attention because stones can chip or crack if water is too hot or if they are struck. Mountings need to be checked regularly and repaired by a jeweler if loose. Chemical cleaners damage some stones, so again warm water and soap are safest for washing these vessels, using a soft brush for cleaning around the stones when necessary.

Altar guilds have overpolished for years, thereby unwittingly cutting short the life of the lovely vessels in their charge. Polishing with a proven polish only two or three times a year is usually sufficient to keep silver pieces immaculate if they are rubbed with a soft cloth whenever they are washed. Polishing gloves impregnated with jeweler's rouge are helpful for maintaining shine between polishings and for rubbing away finger prints and other marks that soap and water won't eliminate. These gloves are stocked by many jewelry and department stores and often gift and antique shops. Cakes of camphor from a drugstore kept in the closet or safe where the silver is stored are an effective tarnish retardant.

An immovable fireproof safe in the sacristy or elsewhere in the church is essential for good vessel care because churches are not burglar proof or fire proof. In addition to the safe, a meticulous inventory of the church's valuable liturgical possessions is also essential. The inventory should contain a history of each piece, a dated professional appraisal, a photograph beside a standard measure, and a full written description of all distinguishing characteristics— including blemishes. The inventory belongs in a safe deposit box or in the church lawyer's office, not in the church building or the rectory or the home of any parishioner. More details about an inventory are included as Appendix 3.

One concern of altar guilds is that, as traditions in a parish change, many still-usable lovely possessions sit idly on shelves because they have been replaced. They need a new purpose in order to continue being gifts given to the glory of God. Some of these things might well be appreciated in other parishes with other customs, other needs. The oldest might be placed in display cases or given to a historical museum. In some parishes valuable articles no longer of any discernible use have been sold and the money placed in a contemporary continuing memorial, such as a columbarium. Good stewardship for an altar guild includes arranging for the church furnishings of yesterday to be put to another dignified use somewhere else today.

LINENS: THE STORY

In general, the various white covers and cloths used on the altar and other tables and shelves in the sanctuary and the sacristy are known collectively as "linens." This does not mean that they are made of pure linen, for they are often cotton or combinations of cotton, linen, and synthetics. The term is a general one, used for convenience as household linens are called "linens." It refers to **fair linens, corporals, purificators, lavabo** and **baptismal towels, chalice (stiff) palls,** and **postcommunion** and **aumbry veils,** (all the liturgical linens), as well as **cerecloths, covers** for the credence and other shelves and tables, **protectors,** and **dust covers** (which may be colored instead of white). All these are the traditional "church linens." The only mandatory linen, however, is the clean white cloth of the Prayer Book rubric (p. 406). All the others have been added through the years for appearance and practicality. When customs have changed, either generally or locally, linens have also changed—-all but the fair linen!

Although both religious and commercial houses will supply church linens, through the years altar guild women have found great joy and satisfaction in making them, not only for their own parishes but for others, too. Simple or elegant, they are an exceptional gift to the Lord of time and talent . The descriptions of individual linens in the next section of the book include simple directions for making them, not a difficult project. Some books with more detailed directions are included in Appendix 5.

All church linens may be made of any firm white material that meets requirements for the use of the article in terms of weight, weave, and durability. Cotton, pure linen, or a synthetic is acceptable. Although pure linen has been the fabric used from early times, in the United States pure linen is imported, difficult to procure, and relatively expensive. Both yardage and finished articles are often beyond parish budgets. Many other white goods have proved suitable through experimental use, and altar guilds long familiar with the sewing, laundering, and storage qualities of pure linen are now becoming familiar with those qualities in cottons and synthetics. These other materials differ markedly, and they all differ from linen. Testing a sample according to its intended use before buying an appreciable quantity is important. Consider the following questions. Is the cloth easy to sew and embroider? Can common stains be completely removed? Does it maintain whiteness? Does it launder well? Is it fire resistant? Is it durable? Cotton that has been combined with polyester is a popular choice because it meets these requirements and is considerably less expensive than pure linen.

Linen, cotton, and synthetics all come in many widths and textures. Cloth used for church sewing is a fine weave, wide-width material available in several weights. In the past, needleworkers have considered it important to use different weights of linen (light, medium, and heavy) for specific pieces. But medium weight material is practical for all of them and prevents waste.

Sources of material sometimes overlooked are the linen closets in the sacristy and in parish homes. Plain white tablecloths, unused or no longer used but in good condition, can be remade into small linens. Fine linen, cotton, or lace handkerchiefs can find new use as aumbry veils or miniature linens for private communion sets or stole protectors. Remnants from cutting standard-sized linens may be the right size for cutting smaller pieces. White birdseye, linen, or fine huck hand towels can be remade into baptismal, lavabo, or sacristy towels—all good fabrics for those pieces because they are absorbent. The strongest parts of any worn larger church linens (including albs, amices, and surplices) may be cut out and remade into smaller ones. Embroideries can be removed from worn linens (leaving a turn-under edge when cutting) and appliquéd onto new ones using fine stitches or couching down with perle cotton. Old lace pieces can be turned into banding or edging, or artistically arranged together on suitable background material for postcommunion or aumbry veils—or even a festal frontal. Some old pieces of lace and embroidery are so exquisite that determining a way to preserve them for parish posterity to see is worth considering (framing them like pictures, for example).

LINENS: THEIR CARE

In keeping with their general philosophy about tending God's altar and caring for its appointments, altar guild workers handle church linens as gently as they would any other delicate items. Careful laundering and prompt repairing prolong the life of cloth. All church linens, therefore, are usually washed by themselves, by machine on the gentle cycle or by hand, using hot water and soap or a mild detergent. They are rinsed until the water is clear of all soap or detergent. (Borax or washing soda will soften hard water and a cup of white vinegar in the final rinse will remove residual alkalis and soap particles.) Linens are not starched! Common stains can usually be removed by immediate treatment before washing, often by simply rubbing gently with soap or detergent. Books about stain removal are available, and some suggestions about treating common stains are in Appendix 4.

Before trying commercial pre-wash products on a stain, be sure of the quality and ingredients of the product and the properties of the stain and the material. Some products are too strong for the material or ineffectual for the stain. *Using commercial bleaches containing chlorine is not recommended for linens except—well diluted—as a last resort.* Using chlorine requires extreme care because chlorine tends to eat fine fabrics!

Although pure linen can be laundered easily and will last a long time, it yellows with age and infrequent use. Rotating articles and laundering them regularly help them stay fresh and white. Restoring yellowed linen to whiteness is most easily accomplished by the time-tested method of lemon juice, very hot water, and sun-bleaching—or by boiling gently for half an hour in water to which washing soda and a mild soap or detergent have been added.

Lace is durable if washed with a mild cold-water-wash product and ironed carefully while still damp. Lace may also be dried on a flat surface without ironing. The shape of the lace is stretched with the hands and the difficult points carefully pinned down.

Ironing either pure or synthetic linens more than is necessary, especially ironing in folds, increases wear. If the sacristy has a formica counter top or the equivalent, freshly washed wet linen and cotton pieces can be spread taut on the clean surface and smoothed firmly into shape to dry. They can literally be peeled off the formica, folded, and finger-pressed for storage, or stored flat and finger-pressed just before use. Synthetics will dry smooth on a counter, too, but need rinsing with a few drops of fabric softener in the water first. Any hard glass-like surface, horizontal or vertical, can substitute for a formica counter.

Since few sacristies (or homes) have a large enough counter for the above wet method to be used for a fair linen, that piece usually has to be ironed. Refrigerating a freshly washed fair linen in a plastic bag for several hours makes ironing it quite easy. A practical method is to iron the hems on the right side first; turn the linen and

61

iron it completely on the wrong side; turn it and iron it once more on the right side, including the hems, to "polish" it. Embroidery is usually ironed on the wrong side with a towel or other absorbent padding under it. Hems and embroideries have to be thoroughly dry before rolling or folding, so "airing" the linen after ironing may be necessary.

Fair linens and credence or other table covers are better stored rolled than folded because folding inevitably makes creases that weaken the fabric and have to be ironed out. Even when sufficient drawer or closet space allows for it, both flat and hanging storage of these large pieces invites creases. Rollers for everyday use can be improvised from cardboard tubes such as those from fabric and rug stores or from large PVC pipe. Covering these rollers with flannelette or washed muslin keeps the linens clean and prevents slipping. If large linens are rolled right-side down, the ends will curl toward the table when unrolled. If they are rolled right-side up, they can be unrolled into position on the table, and the weight of the hems will make them hang straight. Rolled linens stay fresh when wrapped in tissue paper (plastic "stifles" them!) and stored in a drawer or on a shelf. Especially fine linens, heirlooms or not, demand special attention; rollers, boxes, and tissue treated to protect them and lengthen their life are sold by archival suppliers.

If for some reason it is necessary to fold a fair linen, pad the folds generously with tissue to keep the folds from becoming creases. Folding the linen from both ends to the center several times, padding every fold, works well and reduces the linen to a size convenient for carrying or storing in a drawer or box. A linen so folded can be placed directly in the center of the altar and unfolded into position.

A stitch in time is as important for church linens as it is for any other cloth article. Most even-weave fabrics are easily darned, and small patches can be inconspicuous. Even chalice palls can have new corners appliquéd artistically. The emphasis in church linens is primarily on cleanliness and overall neatness. Slightly noticeable repairs affect neither and are a good economic measure.

When linens have been replaced in one parish, they may still be useful in another. Precious storage space is frequently given to linens that are no longer used but are too good to throw away. Careful sacristy housekeeping involves finding new locations for old linens if possible or disposing of them with dignity by burning or burying.

DISPOSABLES

Disposable "linens" are made from three-ply small paper napkins. They are particularly convenient for hospitals, conventions, summer camps, outdoor chapels, and other places where it is not possible to care properly for regular church linens after use. Disposables are also convenient for home celebrations of the Eucharist and for other occasions when individuals or small groups receive the Sacrament away from the church building.

For years during the middle of this century for a variety of reasons some priests were using plain white paper napkins, paper toweling, or large-sized durable tissues for such occasions, sometimes folding the paper products to resemble the cloth articles. In order to standardize this use of such non-linens and to assure their dignified handling, the Presiding Bishop in 1980 approved the use of disposable purificators and towels (not corporals) for convenience in extraordinary situations. He also approved the method for making them, devised by the National Altar Guild Association.

This method stipulates that disposable purificators and towels be made from standard three-ply napkin stock in a size suitable for the purpose. Three-ply napkins are stronger and more absorbent than two-ply. However, even three-ply material has limited durability, so a large gathering requires an adequate supply. The napkins may be refolded to resemble the cloth articles, if desired. They may be decorated with a cross to distinguish their purpose. Although ironing the old shape out and the new shape in was at first recommended, this step is better omitted because napkin layers tend to separate when ironed and finger-pressing is satisfactory.

It is still possible to use other paper products for purificators and towels if the occasion warrants (an emergency, for example, or a primitive setting). The occasion for making Eucharist always outweighs such specifics as available linens and vessels. But as a dignified substitute for small linens, these paper napkin disposables offer the same solution for general use today that they did twenty years ago.

Disposables are simple to make, easily disposed of by burning or burying, and have solved a real problem in the special liturgical ministries of priests and Lay Eucharistic Ministers.

The brief instructions for making the pieces described in this section are for average sizes and may be adjusted according to circumstances. In making linens the intent in most cases is to cut as many pieces as possible from standard width materials with a minimum of waste. Therefore, fitting the measurements to the yardage at hand within reason is practical. For example, it may be possible to cut two fair linens from a single length of wide material or to cut several different small pieces from one length if they are arranged jigsaw fashion. Specifications given here for hem widths are also average and may be adjusted. Strong hems result from small stitches sewn close together using a fine needle and high quality waxed cotton thread or long-filament polyester-cotton thread. The effort is worth it!

Cerecloth

Historically, a **cerecloth** covered a bare stone altar to protect from dampness the cloths placed on top of it. On a wooden altar a cerecloth protects those cloths from stains. *Cerecloth was heavy waxed* linen, a product no longer being manufactured. Waterproofed white flannelette is a satisfactory substitute and, when used as a cerecloth, can adopt the name for historic significance. Waterproofed cloth may also be placed *over* the frontal top under the fair linen or between the fair linen and the corporal (or both) as a buffer in case of wine spills. A cerecloth, whether waxed linen or waterproofed cloth, is simply cut to size; it is not sewn.

Fair Linen

A fair linen is "the clean white cloth" of the rubric, the table cover for the Eucharist. (*BCP*, p. 406) Whatever the table—indoors or out, improvised or not—a clean white cloth of some sort is spread on it as a cover before the bread and wine are placed on it. This white cloth, even if it is a dinner napkin on temporary duty, is called the "fair linen" of the moment and washed as carefully after its use. In the course of liturgical history, because of prevalent interpretations of the Eucharist or pious reasoning, people have attached one significance or another to the fair linen. But in the first years of the church it was a tablecloth, a white cloth spread by a deacon on the special table around which baptized Christians shared their regular meal with their resurrected Lord. That is what it is today.

Historically, the fair linen was removed and put away after the Eucharist, or it was at least covered to keep it pristine for its special purpose. It was not replaced or uncovered until another Eucharist—even for intervening worship services. Although a fair linen usually has other cloths under it, it may be used alone. Because of the rubric, however, it must be used.

Fair linens are most satisfactory when made of medium- weight material. They may fit the altar top exactly or hang down at the ends (or on all sides) to any length. They are, after all, tablecloths, and even tablecloths for our Lord's Table may vary as those of his people do. The cut size should allow for generous hems, one and a half to two inches at least, because good hems help the linen lie flat and hang straight. Corners are mitered for firmness. Embroidered crosses may mark the four corners and the center of the linen but are not necessary. The overhanging edges may be embroidered simply or elaborately in white or any appropriate color. They may also be edged with lace.

Protector, Dust Cover

A **protector** is placed over the fair linen between services to protect it. A white protector covering the linen at all times between Eucharists, as explained above, was called a "prayer cloth." It in turn was covered with another protector, not necessarily white, called a **dust cover**. The dust cover was removed for services other than the Eucharist, leaving the prayer cloth exposed. Both dust cover and prayer cloth were removed for the Eucharist. This practice was familiar until the mid-twentieth century and is still followed in some parishes. But the general use today is a single protector covering the fair linen.

A protector of any type usually fits the altar top exactly, although it doesn't have to. If a prayer cloth is used, it is probably made of material less fine than the fair linen but finer than the dust cover. In general, however, protectors are commonly made of any good material, white or colored. In some churches matching protectors in a color harmonizing with the church decor cover the main altar, side altars, credence, and other table surfaces. In unusually dusty places, plasticized cloth may be worth considering as suitable "dust cover" material.

Corporal

A **corporal** is a square of medium-weight white fabric that is spread on the altar in the center of the fair linen during the

Eucharist. It serves as a placemat for the bread and the chalice of the eucharistic meal. A corporal may have a square of waterproofed cloth under it in case of wine spills. With today's frequent practice of not placing the chalice on the altar until the Offertory (covered at most with a purificator), a second corporal easily replaces a stiff pall as a cover for the chalice, the paten, or the remnants of the meal during the Eucharist, thereby returning to its role of the nineteenth century and before.

The cut size of a corporal is approximately twenty inches, depending on the depth of the altar. Hems are usually a half-inch deep with mitered corners. A corporal may be embroidered in white or in a pleasant pastel color, the embroidered symbol centered one or two inches above the hem on one edge. (Embroidery in the middle could make a filled chalice tip).

Traditionally, a corporal is folded in thirds with the top side in, so that only the wrong side of the cloth shows when the corporal is folded. Folding the corporal this way allows it to be unfolded into position right-side up on the altar and refolded from that position at the close of the Eucharist, encasing any fragments that may have fallen on it.

Purificator

A **purificator** is a square of medium weight white fabric used to wipe the chalice during the Eucharist. It may be embroidered with a white or a colored symbol in the center. A purificator may also be used as a second corporal in place of a stiff pall or in any other way the priest designates. Purificators are the "extra linens for emergencies"—either for ceremonial use or for "liturgical light housekeeping" (absorbing spilled wine, for example).

A purificator is usually about twelve inches square with hems as small as possible, but the size is really determined by the size of the chalice with which it will be used. A purificator is traditionally folded in thirds, right-side out, into a square. Its folded width should be slightly larger than the diameter of the chalice cup over which it is commonly draped, folded, to keep out dust and insects.

Lavabo and Baptismal Towels

A towel is used during the Eucharist to dry the priest's hands during the ceremony of the lavabo or during Baptism to dry the head of the baptized person as well as the priest's hands. Towels are made of medium-weight white fabric cut twelve by eighteen inches or in any other convenient size. Hems are narrow, side hems narrower than ends, and an embroidered white or colored symbol may be centered an inch or so above the hem on one end. Although the symbols may be keyed to the special use (a shell for Baptism, a cross for lavabo), they don't have to be. Towels are towels and interchangeable. Traditionally, they are folded in thirds lengthwise, then in half, in order to hang easily over the server's wrist.

Chalice Pall (Stiff Pall)

A **chalice pall** is a seven- to nine-inch cardboard or plastic square tightly covered with medium-weight white material. Usually a symbol or a picture, simple or elaborate, is embroidered in white or in color on one side. The cover of a cardboard square is made to be removable for washing; the cover of a plastic square is washed in place and the square stood on end to dry.

As has already been explained in earlier sections of the book, this stiff pall developed early in the twentieth century from the original second corporal, which is now slowly replacing it. In the traditional manner of vesting the vessels for the Eucharist, the pall has been placed on the paten not only to cover the priest's wafer but also to provide a firm base over which to drape the silk chalice veil. It has also been used during the Eucharist as a chalice cover to protect the wine from dust or insects. Because of today's departures from this tradition in the kinds of bread presented, the types of vessels used at the altar, and the manner of placing the vessels on the altar, a soft second corporal or a large purificator, folded or unfolded, or an entirely new linen made to resemble these is more practical as a cover than a stiff pall. Often the bread is now a loaf; the paten, a basket, a bowl, or a platter instead of a plate; the vessels, not nested or even placed on the altar until the Offertory, when the table is set. The purpose of a veil and a stiff pall has disappeared. An altar guild can devise its own linens to cover the elements and the vessels according to what the priest thinks is necessary.

Postcommunion Veil

A **postcommunion veil** is a square of light-weight fabric the size of a corporal. It is sometimes used to drape the chalice and paten on the altar if they are not cleansed immediately after the Communions or removed at that time to the credence or the sacristy.

This veil may also be used to cover any consecrated elements that have been removed from the altar.

Use of a postcommunion veil is optional; a second corporal or a large purificator or another similar cloth will serve the same purpose. The size of the veil depends on the size of the chalice it will cover, with allowance for hems and mitered corners. Embroidery, often quite elaborate, is in the center to distinguish it from a corporal, which is about the same size. A postcommunion veil may be edged with lace or made entirely of lace pieces appliquéd to a backing.

Aumbry or Tabernacle Veil

An **aumbry veil** is a curtain of fine material hung inside the door of an aumbry to veil the opening. Its use is optional.

Credence and other table covers

Covers for small tables and shelves are made of medium-weight white material cut to fit the surfaces they will cover, allowing for hems. They may be plain or embroidered simply on the ends, or edged with lace, or both.

* * *

In many parishes of the Episcopal Church of the nineties, altar guild members or other needlework people have undertaken projects of making church linens. Multiplying books of instruction as well as workshops, often sponsored by parish, diocesan, or national altar guilds, provide a good starting place. As with any other art, practice makes perfect.

CHAPTER 5

Dressing Up

*F*or most of Christian history certain garments have been considered "traditional attire for the clergy," though in the beginning they were simply the ordinary clothing of upper- and middle-class men and women of the Roman world in which early Jewish-Christians lived. The men who presided at the first Christian ceremonies wore what they always wore. Even if they had considered dressing otherwise, dressing like everyone else certainly screened them from the eyes of would-be persecutors in those days of political and religious unrest. As the church grew in respectability and importance and moved out into the world of later centuries and other cultures, these garments became "vestments" because church leaders simply continued to wear them even when they were no longer in style.[20]

These "vestments" can be divided into three groups: a eucharistic group reserved for the leaders (bishops, priests, and deacons); a general liturgical group that the laity also could wear; and eventually a special bishops' group. In the eucharistic group: **alb** (an indoor tunic); **amice** (a collar); **girdle** (a belt or a rope); **maniple** (a napkin for the wrist); **chasuble** (an outer garment); **pallium** or **orarium** (a scarf, which centuries later became the emblem of office and was called a **stole**).

In the bishop's group: **rochet** (an extraordinary alb); **chimere** (a sleeveless gown), **scarf** (a long tippet); and the insignia of a bishop—**mitre** (a fabric crown); **crozier** (a shepherd's crook); and **ring** (the emblem of office).

In the general group: **cassock** (a long indoor or outdoor, under or over, coat-like garment); various **capes** with or without **hoods**; a **tippet** (a scarf); **surplice, cotta, dalmatic, and tunicle** (all related to the alb); and several **hats**.

Church functionaries had ample wardrobes! These garments set them apart in the midst of continually changing fashions. Like any other uniform, the costume designated the function and was considered "proper."

All three lines of liturgical wear have been adopted and adapted, added to and subtracted from, by clergy through subsequent centuries according to the customs and resources of their times and places. Although their "daily wardrobe" of the early years stayed the same, there is evidence that leaders reserved their "best clothes" for Sunday. They also set aside different sets of garments for different roles in the liturgy. When the clothing became "vesture," it was progressively decorated with symbols, at first simply and then more elaborately—adding to the visual learning aids already developing in other church furnishings. When knowledge of the historical origin of the garments had faded from actual memory and become folklore, allegorical ideas and some religious meanings were thought of for many of them. The ideas and meanings were designed to intensify religious experience or to teach, but they were entirely imaginative. Now on the brink of the twenty-first century, some of those legends still cling to old vestments. As *The Westminster Dictionary* suggests, they probably need to be examined as to their "relevance and effectiveness in the total communication pattern of worship."[21]

Over the years, different fabrics, patterns, colors, decorations, and even combinations of garments have been used as vesture, but the lineage has always been obvious. The old Roman everyday clothing has contributed to the contemporary formal dress of Christian clergy of all peruasions, if only in their "basic blacks." It is particularly recognizable in the attire of clergy in the "one, holy, catholic, and apostolic" tradition. But even in this one tradition variation of all sorts has been rampant.

The Church of England tried at times, officially and unofficially, to introduce some degree of uniformity into vestment wear, with much discussion and little success. The Episcopal Church, at its beginning, set the parameters for vestments and all other phases of ceremonial by stating in the first sentence of the preface to the first *Book of Common Prayer* (1789):

> It is a most invaluable part of that blessed "liberty wherewith Christ hath made us free," that in his worship different forms and usages may without offence be allowed, provided the substance of the Faith be kept entire. (*BCP*, 1979, p. 9)

In the 1870s the Episcopal Church made a futile attempt to exercise some control of clerical dress, but the spirit of that first preface carried.[22] Today canon law says nothing about vestment wear—about type, material, design, or occasion, and the rubrics in *The Book of Common Prayer* say very little.

On the other hand, in every period and every locale of the Anglican Communion in the United States and elsewhere, much has been said as a result of changed concepts of beauty, new research by liturgical leaders, constant development of new materials, innovative ideas of commercial and amateur vestment makers, and demands of the climate and the economy. Often local groups of worshipers with strong ideas and attitudes have added an influential voice. The ensuing array of garments that has been created has given leaders of all orders a wide range from which to choose whatever dress they and their congregations can be comfortable with. The dress they pick out will at best enhance worship and give anonymity to those presiding. Color, material, and design do this only when they keep the attention of worshipers, priest and people alike, focused on the glory of God.

Well-documented books and tracts about the history of vestments are available for people interested in tracing the particulars of change.[23] Some of them are fascinating, the illustrations in particular. But it is enough for most worshipers today to understand that change is to be expected, that it happens all the time, and that there is little right or wrong in vestments. Only the clergy wear stoles and chasubles; only a bishop wears bishop's vesture. Otherwise, within the few confines of the rubrics, choices and changes are allowable, locally and regularly. An altar guild's responsibility is to learn to care for, perhaps even to make, the garments each of its successive priests chooses to wear, knowing that all priests have different ideas and that those ideas are bound to vary widely.

VESTMENTS: CHOICES AND COLORS

The first choice a priest makes is among the different categories of vestments. Practical questions follow, such as tradition, budget, climate, and decor in the parish where the vestments will be worn. And then the priest can consider fabrics, colors, and ornamentation.

All liturgical vestments may be worn by men and women alike: "his and hers" pertains only to size because women tend to be more diminutive than men. Commercial vestment catalogs provide two standard size charts, one for men and one for women. Handmade vestments can be designed for both, with an eye to individual size and fit as well as the usual questions about style, material, color, and adornment. Contemporary pattern-making aids and techniques as well as materials open boundless possibilities to creative vestment makers!

As in the case of hangings, materials for vestments have always tended to be the best that people could afford among those suitable for the purpose. "Suitable" now includes consideration of comfort, care, and durability. The idea that any one material could be "proper" or "improper" has no historical basis. Whatever material makes up best into a particular garment, all things considered, is the "proper" material for it. Diversity of material has existed from parish to parish, even within one parish, from generation to generation. Twentieth-century fabrics simply add to that diversity. So in sacristies today elegant vestments made years ago from brocade and tapestry, wool and linen, in seasonal colors, and embroidered or appliquéd with classic symbols and ornate designs, hang side by side with comparably beautiful vestments created from wrinkle-free, easy-care, durable, lightweight, washable, "miracle" fabrics in a wide range of colors appliquéd or embroidered in simple contemporary designs.

Colors from the entire spectrum are now being used, just as they were in the late Middle Ages. Before that time, color of vestments was not a crucial matter. Actually, until then, clergy are reported to have preferred white. But once colors were introduced in the church, a whole new world opened up. The emphasis obviously switched to beautifying the service of worship with cloth and needle in all the loveliest ways possible, following no particular color system, even using many colors at once. Restrictions had to do with reserving the best for the greatest feasts, whatever the color.

At the outset in many churches red, blood red, was the year-round color for everything. With the passage of time people began to associate colors with life. White and gold stood for purity and festivity; green and yellow, for growth and energy; purple, for royalty; red, for blood, for courage, for martyrdom; light blue, for hope; dark blue and violet, for penitence; and black, for grief. By the twelfth century different colors were associated with different occasions in the life of the church and appeared in vestments and hangings for those occasions. The practice spread—and varied greatly.

Finally, in the 1570s under Pope Gregory, Rome systematized the different color uses with a rubric that spelled out a standard sequence geared symbolically to church seasons and holy days. Some variation was possible because of alternate colors and shades. But the familiar white, green, violet, red, and black of Western church calendars stemmed from that rubric.

The church in England used these colors until the Reformation. In the years after that, "church colors" slid out of favor. They represented an undesirable closeness with Rome. Although some clergy continued to use them, the Anglican Communion was basically black and white in dress for all occasions from 1600 to 1850.

Then in the mid-nineteenth century, in both the Church of England and the Episcopal Church, a movement to restore full eucharistic dress and the five-color sequence began. It progressed steadily throughout the twentieth century. Commercial vestment houses and church calendars with dates printed in colors assisted the movement. However, church calendars don't control the church, and vestment houses are not official in any way. So in this last decade of the twentieth century some priests still prefer to preside in black and white (cassock and surplice)—with a colored stole. Nevertheless, the overall trend in vestments today is toward a wide variety of color in material and design. The common alternate hues of the Roman sequence are amplified by all the imaginable shades of those colors. Clergy clothing has definitely achieved a new dimension!

VESTMENTS: THEIR CARE AND STORAGE

The care of vestments requires local solutions. They have to be kept as clean and neat as any ordinary clothes in which people dress up for special occasions. A stitch in time, immediate spot removal, frequent touch-ups with an iron, careful storage—all these prolong the life of vestments and keep them presentable.

Laundering, dry cleaning, and repairing depend on the fabric, age, and value of the garments as well as the number, time, and skill of altar guild workers. Polyester is one challenge; brocade, another. New and old fabrics require different treatment. So common good housekeeping sense needs to be tempered by knowing the materials to be cared for. A few vestments can be washed out and hung to drip-dry in some sacristies, but most need to be taken to more spacious home laundries or commercial launderers or dry cleaners known for good work with fine garments. Major mending tasks need expert hands, as do major cleaning tasks. If mending projects require more skill than is available locally, several convents, historical societies, textile museums, and diocesan altar guilds are possible sources of help.[24]

As for storage, small vestments and "accessory items" such as cinctures can easily be kept in drawers, but most major vestments last longer if kept on padded hangers, preferably in separate garment bags. Some sacristies have generous closets to accommodate these. Other sacristies have built-in banks of racks over which chasubles will hang, or large shallow drawers in which they can be laid flat with tissue to cushion embroidery and unavoidable folds.

But many sacristies have limited space, and altar guilds in such places have to improvise because vestments depend on careful storage for long life. Fixed or movable closets elsewhere in the church building will serve this purpose. In old churches, closets and chests were often incorporated into the decor of the nave, handsome wood carving on doors or panels masking the hidden storage space. Occasionally, an altar was moved out from the east end of a church and an inner wall built across the chancel behind it. This wall screened a space that could be used, not only for storing vestments and hangings, but for vesting as well. Both these inventive storage ideas have been copied in some modern churches.

Vestments more than most other furnishings are inclined to multiply, new ones of all types being added from time to time to replace worn ones or to introduce new materials, new designs, new colors, or new sizes. The space taken up by the ones no longer worn could be put to better use, as could those vestments themselves. Replaced vestments that are still wearable can generally go to new homes and extend their usefulness. Even good ornamentation on badly worn vestments can be carefully removed and preserved for display or transferred to other vestments. Most diocesan altar guilds can help parish guilds with a relocation problem.

Part of the care of vestments is awareness of their value in case an emergency forces replacement. Vestments are expensive! An item-by-item illustrated inventory with regularly updated descriptions and appraisals is just as essential for vestments as for vessels. On an inventory it is important to indicate the ownership of each vestment: is it the church's or the priest's? Frequently, some items kept in a sacristy are the personal property of a priest and leave when the priest leaves. A vestment inventory, like a vessel inventory, belongs in a safe deposit box or in the church lawyer's office, not in the church building or in private hands.

Just as the first step for people wishing to donate vestments is to consult the priest in charge, so is consultation with the priest the first step for people interested in making vestments. Regardless of what may be in use elsewhere, the priest in charge of a parish at any given time is the final authority on what is appropriate and what will be used there. With the priest's approval of the intended design, style, and material for any vestment, however, people who are interested can make a significant gift of time and talent by creating vestments.

Kits of precut material available from some commercial vestment makers or diocesan altar guilds are perhaps a good place for beginners to start. The expert cutting and careful instructions will lead to a presentable first product and give the producer a feeling of confidence. Men and women who are more adventuresome and want to make garments "from whole cloth" will discover in bookstores and libraries many excellent books of instruction about all steps of ecclesiastical needlework. Appendix 5 contains an annotated list of some of these books. Regional chapters of the Embroiderers Guild of America sometimes offer classes and workshops for anyone interested in learning about embroidery. And several vestment makers and diocesan altar guilds provide workshops in the basics of vestment making (including patterns, cinctures, and mitres).

The People of God have different gifts to offer, different talents to put to work. Stitchery is one of these. The diversity of materials and colors and designs constantly coming into use in the church beckons those whose love for God can be expressed with a needle. The church is ready for them liturgically, both men and women, and strongly encourages them to participate in the creation of vestments. Today's understanding of the "work of the people" in worship involves far more than taking part in worship services.

When eucharistic vestments were reintroduced in the nineteenth century, they rejoined the black-and-white attire that had become customary. By 1960 the three distinct groups of the early days were back in much of the Episcopal Church, fitting into their former roles: eucharistic vestments with their historic names (see above), general liturgical ("choir") vestments, and bishops' attire.

Shifts in liturgical practice and vestment design after 1960 fuzzied that distinction. Current models of most historic vestments were still in use but not always and not everywhere. Some familiar old ones were disappearing (the maniple, for instance), and some imaginative new ones soon began to appear as combinations of three or more of the old (the cassock-alb). The whole assortment will be described in these pages because part of altar guild expertise is vestment recognition.

With the addition of a **cassock-alb** (a combined cassock, amice, and alb) and a **chasuble-alb** (a combined cassock, amice, alb, and chasuble) to vestment closets in the late twentieth century, many of the "old" vestments have become in a sense "optional." Not the stole, because a stole is the mark of priesthood, but the others.

For choir vesture today a priest may wear a cassock-alb with or without a girdle instead of the familiar cassock and surplice. A bishop may wear one, too, instead of rochet and chimere. The priest's tippet and hood and the bishop's scarf are not often seen. As for Eucharist, the choice is much wider.

The only rubrics in *The Book of Common Prayer* pertaining to vestments are in "Episcopal Services," primarily in the ordination rites. They stipulate vesture for a new bishop, priest, or deacon at that time (bishop: pp. 511, 521, 552; priest: pp. 524, 534, 553; deacon: pp. 536, 545, 554). These rubrics alone specify garments for ecclesiastical functions. Besides a stole, the clergy choose their vestments for all other worship occasions according to order of ministry and taste, their judgment tempered by local conditions and customs.

A priest may choose to dress in the full complement of six eucharistic vestments, either "traditional" or contemporary in cut, fabric, and design. A priest may also preside at the Eucharist in cassock, surplice, and stole; a bishop in rochet, chimere, and scarf or stole; or either one of them in cope, alb (with or without a girdle), and stole (as has been the custom in the Anglican communion through much of its history.) A priest or a bishop may also preside at a holy table in street dress with a stole, a practice common in informal settings. With the additional "all-in-one" vestments now available, a priest may wear chasuble-alb and stole; cassock-alb (with or without a girdle), stole, and chasuble; cassock-alb with just a stole; or cassock-alb, stole, and cope. Some priests are fairly consistent about their vesture, but others like variety.

The altar guild's task in any setting—indoors or out, formal or informal, at home or away, in "God's house" or the world's—is to devise a workable plan for having ready, before any service, whatever vestments the priest plans to wear. At one time, in addition to the diagram for vesting a chalice described earlier, every sacristy had a diagram for "laying out" the vestments. The usual six were arranged on a table in order of donning them, the last one (the chasuble) on the bottom (see Appendix 6). That diagram is not particularly useful now. The fabrics and construction of most of today's garment-like vestments fare better hanging than laid out and can be just as convenient on hangers as on a table. (In truth, most of yesterday's lovely old fabrics are also better hung than laid out!) Today elegant old-fabric or modern new-fabric chasubles, chasuble-albs, cassock-albs, and copes often remain on hangers until donned. The amice, alb, and cassock are now incorporated into the cassock-alb, the girdle seldom needed, and the maniple almost never worn. Often the only vestment left to be "laid out" today is the stole!

The altar guild's principal responsibility is the rector's vestments, but others may also be in their charge. Some parishes have several priests on the staff to vest or whose personal vestments may be in the sacristy. Extra vestments may be kept in the sacristy for visiting clergy. These also have to be cared for and ready when needed. The altar guild's "workable plan" may become complicated if several priests are involved in one service. But part of the joy of worship is the joy in planning for it, and the joy in watching it happen.

VESTMENTS: ONE BY ONE[25]

Cassocks

Whether or not **cassocks** are considered to be "vestments" in the strict sense, they certainly have vested all official participants in church services from the beginning—choir, layreaders, crucifers, acolytes, servers, and all orders of clergy. The original cassocks were the Roman citizen's basic black floor-length tunics that church leaders wore when the church began and their successors have worn in one form or another ever since. Until the mid-nineteenth century cassocks were street dress for clergy, and only recently have they ceased being the basic undergarments for all other liturgical vestments.

Cassock	*Cassock*	*Cassock*
Anglican	Roman	Jesuit

Cassocks for priests and deacons are still black, but those for lay assistants may be any color appropriate for the place. Cassocks for a bishop and the whole cathedral staff are normally purple. Sometimes the purple is limited to purple piping and buttons on black. Sometimes two purples prevail: blue-purple in the cathedral, red-purple outside.

Cassocks today are made in three styles, all full-length, close-fitting, long-sleeved, deep-cuffed, and high-necked, with a front-opening mandarin neckline designed to be worn with "clerical" collars. The Latin (Roman) style zips or buttons center front, neck to hem. The Anglican style overlaps fully in front; it fastens at the waist and both shoulders with snaps, buttons, or velcro. The Jesuit style overlaps partially in front, fastening at the center waist and the neck. All three styles may be belted with a matching rope or sash (girdle/cincture) or a leather belt.

An interesting bit of cassock history (not a legend) is that in the Middle Ages in cold climates cassocks were lined with wool such as sheepskin or were topped with full gowns of fur (*pellicea*) to make bearable the long hours clergy spent in churches. As a result, northern cassocks became so bulky that the usual albs wouldn't fit over them and had to be enlarged. Thus surplices came into being. *Surplice* comes from *super pelliceum*, "over fur."

Surplice

Originally a wide-sleeved extra-large alb, the **surplice** appeared in the twelfth century as explained above. Cassock and surplice have been liturgical choir dress ever since, cold climate or not. During the approximately three centuries when eucharistic vestments were not acceptable in the Church of England and the Episcopal Church, surplice and cassock were eucharistic dress as well. With a stole, they still may be that.

In the beginning a surplice was full and plain, long with huge sleeves, very like some albs pictured in mosaics of the sixth-century church. Over the years the hem has gone up and down; the sleeves have been wide and narrow; the neck has been round and square; the body has been full and skimpy; and the front has been plain or embroidered. It has even been decorated with lace. But surplices have always been white.

Cotta

Early surplice

Contemporary surplice

Today surplices are generally made from *any* easy-care white material that will drape and launder well. They are cut very full, usually hang from a round yoke, and extend to well below the knee. They may be embroidered or otherwise decorated, usually center front.

Cotta

A **cotta** is an abbreviated version of a surplice: it has a shorter body, shorter round sleeves, and a round or square yoke. Cottas have been worn over cassocks by choir, acolytes, servers, and crucifers for centuries but not customarily by other lay assistants or by clergy in the Church of England or the Episcopal Church. Today the cotta-cassock combination is being replaced by cassock-albs, even for children.

Tippet and Hood

Originally the black **tippet** (scarf) was probably part of the **hood** worn with a black gown as everyday clothing in medieval universities. Later the two were separated, but "tippet and hood" became part of

clergy choir dress in the Church of England
and the Episcopal Church. Neither is worn
for the Eucharist because both represent
personal academic achievement.

A **hood** is worn around the neck hanging down the back. Its length denotes academic degree, the colored silk lining
denotes university or seminary, the colored velvet banding denotes field of study.

Tippet

A *tippet* is worn around the neck like a scarf, lying over the hood at
the shoulders. It is wide, usually pleated at the neck for fit and decorated on the ends with emblems of church or school. A tippet
may be worn without a hood.

Amice

The word *amicio* means to wrap around. An amice is a rectangle
(sometimes a square) of white cloth with long string ties which
wrap around the waist. It is usually plain, but it may have an
apparel (a strip of other material matching similar apparels
attached to the alb) or an embroidered collar.

Amices

An amice, worn from the sixth century, became an official
eucharistic vestment in the eighth. At the outset, an amice was
wrapped around the neck like a kerchief to give a collar effect to the
other vestments and protect them from sweat. For years it was
donned *after* the alb. But in the tenth century when long hair styles
were fashionable, placing it on the head like a hood *before* assum-
ing the other vestments protected the vestments until they were in
place, and it could be adjusted to collar position to return to its
original purpose.[26] Cassock-albs eliminate the need for amices.

Alb

Albs are descended from the white Roman under-tunic, the *tunica alba*, a white, straight-cut, sleeveless, collarless garment of mid-
calf length with a short, buttoned front neck opening. It was belted with a rope or a cincture. In the third century the alb added tight

or full sleeves (*tunica manicata alba*); by the fifth century it became floorlength (*tunica talaris*) in order to cover the cassock under it. Albs in one form or another were worn over cassocks by all Christian leaders for all services from the end of the first century until the twelfth century when surplices began to replace them. Albs have had times of elegance (colored silk, lace, embroidery), times of simplicity (plain white linen or wool). The custom of sometimes decorating them at front and back hems and cuffs with "apparels" (see "Amice") originated in the eleventh century. Modern albs are plain, made like the *tunica talaris*, of any durable white fabric usually easy-care.

Alb   *Alb with amice, girdle and stole*

During the early centuries the whiteness of albs was emphasized, and church leaders were told to keep them especially clean. That whiteness endowed them with many pious significances, such as purity, simplicity, and baptismal unity with Christ. So even though they were originally just the early Roman white tunic, the aura of being "clothed with Christ" has clung to albs (and to all other white ceremonial garments) to this day.

Cassock-Alb

Modern **cassock-albs** are white or off-white, made in a variety of easy-care materials. They incorporate the cassock shape with the alb/surplice white (although it may also be off-white) and the amice neck-band (in a stand-up collar or a soft hood). They may be belted with girdle or cincture. A cassock-alb does not need a cassock under it.

For the sacraments, priests may wear cassock-albs with stoles. Addition of a chasuble or a dalmatic or a tunicle is optional. Plain cassock-albs are suitable choir dress for all clergy and for lay assistants in all services—white in the sanctuary and white or colored in the choir.

Cassock-alb—front and back

Girdle/Cincture

Today the terms **girdle** and **cincture** are interchangeable for the long cord and the wide band (sash) used to belt an alb or a cassock. First-century Roman dress included a cord girding the under tunic. In early church terminology, a *girdle* was the cord; a *cincture*, the band. Most old altar guild manuals follow this distinction.

The sash girds an Anglican cassock; the cord girds an alb; but either may be worn with the other cassocks or with the cassock-alb. Both rope and band match the garments they gird. A leather belt, black or brown, is sometimes used with black cassocks. The band fastens snugly around the waist with hooks or snaps and is made with sash ends. The cord is worn doubled with either alb or cassock and is long enough for the ends to hang below the knee.

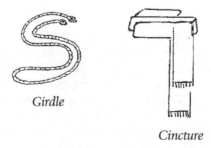

Girdle

Cincture

Stole

A **stole** is a long narrow neck scarf worn by ordained clergy when presiding or assisting at the Eucharist or other sacraments. It is the emblem of their ordination. A deacon wears a stole over the left shoulder, the ends either hanging straight front and back or crossing the body to be secured in some way under the right arm. A priest wears a stole around the neck, the ends either hanging straight in front or crossed on the breast to be held in place by a girdle. A bishop wears a stole hanging straight in front. The stole goes either over or under the chasuble or the dalmatic, or over the surplice, the cassock-alb, or the chasuble-alb.

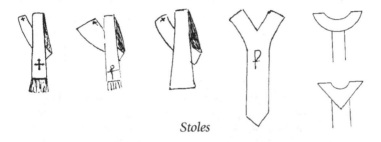

Stoles

Stoles have varied over the centuries from very long to very short, from narrow to wide to contoured. They have been white or colored; linen, silk, wool, cotton, or other fabrics; plain or elaborate with embroidery, braid, and fringe. Before the Roman color sequence was adopted, it was usual for stole and maniple to match (and to match orphreys and apparels) but to be in contrast to other vestments. Today's stoles are made of many fabrics and in all colors. They do not necessarily match any other vestments and often are neutral or multicolored so they will blend with all. Some are hand-woven, most are decorated with classic or contemporary designs, embroidered or appliquéd simply or elaborately on the ends or along the entire length. Stoles vary in shape and length. Some contemporary models are quite stylized. Generally speaking, however, they are long and wide and traditional enough in cut to make a clear statement of what they are—the emblem of priesthood.

Today's *pallium stole* is a circle of cloth that fits around the neck and has long wide strips hanging center front and back. Its origin is debatable, but it probably descends from a white wool scarf common to bishops in the fifth century and worn similarly—looped

83

around the neck, the ends hanging front and back. The use of scarves (this **pallium** by a bishop, an **orarium** by a priest or deacon) spread. By the twelfth century the name stole had been given to both. Stoles had become the priestly mark of office. In the Church of England, between Elizabeth I and the return of vestments in the nineteenth century, stoles were not favored. Since then, however, they have again become the essential liturgical vestment for priests.

Maniple

A **maniple** is a short narrow scarf that loops around the left wrist and matches the stole in material, ornamentation, and color. Maniples are seldom worn today.

A maniple goes back to the *mappa*, a useful napkin or handkerchief that a Roman citizen carried in his hand because he had no pockets. It eventually became an emblem of authority for a Roman consul, who carrried it in his right hand (and threw it down for the games to start.) Maniples have been part of Christian vesture for the Eucharist since the seventh or eighth century. For some centuries they, too, were practical napkins carried in the hand by all clerics. Eventually a maniple became just an ornament for the left wrist and only for clergy down to the rank of sub-deacon. Today it is generally held to be a superfluous vestment.

Chasuble

The word **chasuble** comes from the Latin *casula*, "little house" or tent, a descriptive word for the wholly enveloping conical outer cloak, the *paenula*, which everyone wore in the Graeco-Roman world and which church leaders continued to wear when worldly fashions changed. A chasuble is the outer eucharistic vestment.

The historic chasuble/paenula was conical, made from a half-circle of wool fabric with a radius of approximately sixty inches. The cut edges of the circle were folded together to meet in a front seam, the top point cut slightly to make an opening for the head. (Because a chasuble was intended to be a tent and envelop the wearer from neck to hands and ankles, that sixty inches didn't allow for much variation in the height of wearers!) The front seam (the back, too, if quarter circles were joined to form a half) was reinforced and hidden with narrow strips of cloth or braid called **orphreys** (*aurum*, gold and *Phrygius*: "Phrygian gold") because gold was woven in. (All such strips added to vesture were/are called orphreys, gold or not.) When at a later time the chasuble was rotated, shifting the seams to the sides, the orphreys remained front and back as pure decoration—eventually with added arms to give them a cross shape.

At first all clergy wore chasubles (probably white wool), but gradually the use became limited to the chief celebrant at the Eucharist. In the tenth century, when the clergy were growing in importance and the church was becoming wealthy, chasubles of colored silk appeared in place of the familiar white wool. They were embroidered and quite elegant, but they remained conical—full and tentlike.

Historic chasuble shapes
earliest chasuble shape

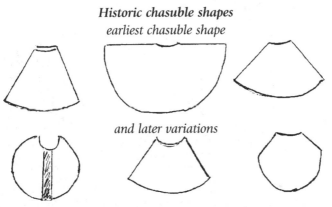

and later variations

Then in the thirteenth century the "cone," the tent, gave way to a change in ceremonial. The celebrant standing back to the people was required to raise the Host above his head with both hands during the consecration so that all the worshipers behind him could see it. Freeing his hands from the conical chasuble to do this was possible but difficult, so the "cone" was cut away at the sides to facilitate the action. One cut led to another, and after almost a thousand years of being basically one shape and one size, chasubles in the next four centuries changed in both shape and size dozens of times from country to country and era to era. They also became more ornate in fabric and embellishment— tapestry, brocade, velvet, and cloth of gold and silver as well as intricate embroidered designs often using jewels and goldwork. They became works of art more than vestments.[27]

After the Reformation and the "black-and-white period" of the

Church of England and the Episcopal Church mentioned earlier, simpler chasubles were among the vestments reintroduced in the mid-nineteenth century. And simpler chasubles prevail at the end of the twentieth. Closer in shape to the earliest ones, less ornate than the intervening ones, today's chasubles are made of many materials besides traditional silks and wools. Most of them are practical in terms of care, comfort, and climate. They may be any color at all, multicolored or neutral. They may be plain or decorated with modern designs or traditional symbols using any skills of clothwork. Orphreys may be placed in old or new patterns or omitted entirely. Good taste, the priest's wishes, and a desire to beautify worship effectively are the only restrictions to imagination in creating modern chasubles that make a statement.

Contemporary chasubles

Cope and Cape

A **cope** is actually a full, open-front, conical chasuble fastened on the breast with a large and often jeweled velvet or metal clasp called a *morse*. In Roman days a cope was an outer (*cappa*, top) outdoor garment with a functional hood. In black wool it was the *cappa nigra* and still is today—the black wool cape (with hood) worn for outdoor ceremonies in cold weather by clergy (or others) wearing choir vestments.

Sixth-century mosaics and seventh-century records show that copes had become ecclesiastical vesture by that time. A ceremonial cope was and is customarily made of rich fabric in brilliant colors (tapestry, brocade, velvet, cloth of gold), but it need not be. A cope has usually been ornamented with tassels, fringe, braid, jewels or orphreys in various designs. A wide orphrey around the neck and down both sides of the front is common. The hood long ago ceased to be functional, but a simulated one is generally attached to the back. Modern copes are still elegant vestments, but their elegance tends to be in fine fabric more than in ornamentation.

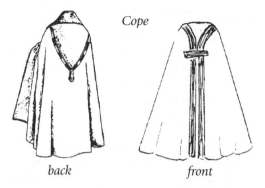

Cope

back   front

Copes are not exclusively episcopal vestments, although they have normally been so costly that in many dioceses only a cathedral could afford one. Copes, therefore, have been popularly associated with bishops who often wear "cope and mitre" at their cathedrals in processions and sometimes in episcopal services. But *any participant may wear a cope in procession in any parish,* and a priest (or deacon) may wear a cope as the outer vestment for any service if its fullness isn't a deterrent. A cope has been an alternate eucharistic vestment in England since the Reformation, but that practice has only recently appeared in the Episcopal Church.

Chasuble-Alb

Chasuble-alb is one of several names for an all-in-one eucharistic vestment. White or off-white with large sleeves and a hood, it is a composite cassock-alb-amice, but it is also full and seamed in the front to resemble the chasuble. A chasuble-alb is worn with a stole on top—its principal decoration. Priests who travel between parishes, who live in warm climates, or who preside in informal settings or as concelebrants find these garments especially useful.

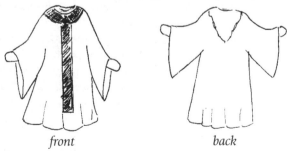

front   back

Chasuble-alb (with pallium stole)

87

Dalmatic and Tunicle

Dalmatic and **tunicle** are lesser eucharistic vestments than the chasuble. They both are wide-sleeved over-tunics, related to the shorter alb, originally white wool or linen worn over the alb for a second layer of clothing. Though basically alike, they were slightly different. Dalmatics, for example, had *clavi* over the shoulders (strips of fabric similar to apparels). Tunicles didn't, and tunicles were shorter than dalmatics.

In frescoes and mosaics church leaders of different rank are pictured in dalmatics. But in the ninth century the dalmatic was assigned to the deacon (the gospeler) and the tunicle to the sub-deacon (the epistoler, lay or ordained). Even so, lesser participants in the Eucharist, such as the crucifer, sometimes wore a tunicle, and some bishops are pictured wearing *both*, with cassock and alb underneath and a chasuble on top! When a bishop happened to be the epistoler at a Eucharist, he would wear a tunicle to indicate his function at the time—just as a bishop or a priest today, serving as deacon for the Eucharist, often (correctly) wears a stole over the left shoulder fastened under the right arm, deacon-style, to indicate the role.

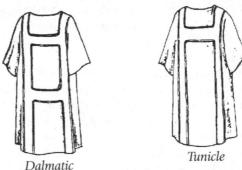

Dalmatic   Tunicle

Dalmatics and tunicles today are matched to the chasuble worn at the same Eucharist. They are squared at the hem, slit at the sides below the waist, sleeved, and decorated with ladderlike orphreys as in the illustration. The tunicle is slightly less everything than the dalmatic. They are no longer required eucharistic dress but may be worn (dalmatic for the role of deacon, tunicle for sub-deacon). However, because deacons now commonly vest simply in just cassock and surplice or in cassock-alb and stole and epistolers tend to be unvested members of the congregation, these two garments (if a parish owns them) usually appear only on festive occasions.

BISHOP'S REGALIA

Rochet, Chimere, and Scarf

A **rochet** is a derivative of the alb. It is an enveloping long white garment worn under a **chimere**, ungirded, with or without a cassock. A rochet has two styles. One form is quite similar to the alb, long and not too full with straight sleeves. The more usual form is ample in body, as a surplice is, but hangs to the feet. The sleeves of this second form are full and long, gathered at the wrist and secured with either stiff fluted cuffs and a narrow red or black ribbon or narrow straight cuffs and a wider red or black band. The ribbon matches the chimere. The cuffs are usually detachable to simplify laundering. In the past, fabric for a rochet has been lawn or fine linen. But any good quality white material that will drape well is suitable, preferably an easy-care variety.

The rochet was first worn by clergy in general and by lay people assisting at the liturgy. Toward the end of the Middle Ages it became reserved for bishops and some other dignitaries. At that time it was narrow-sleeved or sleeveless. The *huge* sleeves developed in the Church of England after "rochet and chimere" were designated "episcopal dress" in the time of Elizabeth I. At one time the sleeves worn by Anglican bishops in England and the United States were so full that they were attached to the chimere instead of the rochet!

Chimere　　　*Rochet*　　　*Scarf*

The *chimere* is a scarlet or black academic gown like that for a person with a doctorate, only sleeveless. Although traditionally silk or satin, a chimere may be made of any substantial material according to preference. It is worn over a rochet, may be topped by a *scarf*, a long version of a tippet. "Rochet and chimere" appeared in the church in the Middle Ages and (as noted above) became liturgical and civil dress for bishops in England in the sixteenth century.

A bishop may preside at the Eucharist in church in either rochet, chimere, and scarf (or stole) or in alb, chasuble (or cope), and stole—with a mitre, if desired. A bishop is vested at ordination to preside at *that* Eucharist according to the basic garment worn for the rite, an alb or a rochet. In informal situations (at conferences, camps, or meetings, for example) a bishop may preside in cassock and surplice, or cassock-alb, or street dress—all with a stole, as any other priest may.

Ring, Crozier, and Mitre

The **ring, crozier,** and **mitre** are the usual and time-honored emblems of the office of bishop. They are the three listed in the rubric in *The Book of Common Prayer* (p. 553). The Prayer Book, however, is permissive in this as in most instances, and allows for "other suitable gifts." A pectoral cross may be and sometimes is one of these, although anyone may wear a pectoral cross.

Since the sixth or seventh century in the Western church, a **ring** has been given to a new bishop in the ordination rite as a sign of office. The ring is a signet ring bearing the bishop's personal seal. Of precious metal, it is usually set with an amethyst, the traditional color for bishops, and is worn on the third finger of the right hand. Signet rings were common to people in positions of authority at the time the church began, so when the Church became "legal" in the fourth century, bishops automatically became "persons in positions of authority." Eventually the ring attested to that.

In the beginning the bishop's **crozier** was just a staff, a walking stick—hence the name *pastoral staff* which the English gave it much later. *Crozier* means "crook bearer." In those early days many people walked with a staff, bishops among them. Although not a vestment, a staff gradually became part of a bishop's outfit. By the seventh century in some places, by the ninth in most, a new bishop was given one at consecration as a sign of office. During the next centuries, the crozier changed several times in length and in the shape of the head. One form was the fairly tall crook, which by the thirteenth century was the shape accepted for bishops in the West. Whether the association with sheep and shepherds came before or after the crook was adopted is a matter of conjecture, but it is an excellent example of the attachment of allegory to a piece of church furnishing.

In procession and for ceremonial occasions a bishop carries a crozier in the left hand with the crook top facing "the flock." The crozier is an emblem of rank, so a bishop's chaplain does *not* carry it or hold it except when the bishop's hands are otherwise involved liturgically. According to Cyril Pocknee, "There is no ancient or proper authority which suggests that bishop[s] may not carry [their] croziers outside [their] diocese[s], or that suffragan bishops may not carry their pastoral staffs in the presence of Archbishops and Diocesan Bishops. The crozier is an emblem of episcopal rank and not one of mere jurisdiction."[28]

The Presiding Bishop and archbishops carry their own croziers because of their rank as bishops. They also have **primatial crosses** or **cross-staffs** because of their jurisdiction. (A primatial cross is a staff topped with a small cross.) The primatial cross *is* carried by a chaplain in procession before the Presiding Bishop or an archbishop who carry their own croziers.

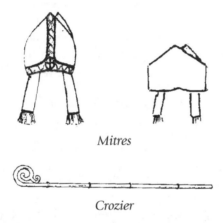

Mitres

Crozier

A **mitre** is a bishop's "crown" or helmet. (The word is Latin for turban.) In the eleventh century some Christian bishops received grants from the Pope to wear mitres, and by the end of the twelfth so many bishops had received these grants that mitres became accepted everywhere as part of the official outfit for bishops. (This development is interesting because all earlier mitrelike headgear among Christians seems to have been worn by deaconesses and abbesses!) Although from that time a mitre became one of the three emblems of office given to a new bishop at consecration, occasionally other church dignitaries have worn them—abbots, for example, and cardinals.

The first mitres were white linen and cone-shaped, but soon both the material and the shape changed. The cone was rounded off, then dented in the middle, resembling the top of a heart. Next, the two rounds of the "heart" were pointed, and then the whole mitre was turned forty-five degrees and became the ancestor of all mitres since—the basic double-pointed hat that is familiar today. Mitres have been linen, velvet, and silk, occasionally gold or silver; they have been plain or elaborately decorated, straight-sided or round, short or tall—all according to a bishop's preference. At the back a mitre has two *lappets*, short "tails" of ribbon), perhaps a vestige of an early mitre that was held in place by a band tied around the head.[29]

A bishop may wear a mitre with chasuble or cope at confirmations or ordinations, in processions, and during parts of the Eucharist. It does not have to match anything. In fact, it is often purposely unmatched so that it may be worn with any chasuble or cope. Mitres were out of use in England for years in the 1700s not only because ceremony was suspect, but because dignitaries wore wigs. When Samuel Seabury, the first American Episcopal bishop, wanted a mitre in 1786, he had to order it from England. English vestment makers, however, had no current models to copy and no patterns to follow either. They had to resort to pictures to create a design for the first mitre of the Episcopal Church![30]

MISCELLANEOUS VESTMENTS

Verger's Gown and Mace

A traditional **verger's gown** resembles an academic gown. The sleeves are distinctive. They hang straight, like wide double-scarves with pointed ends, the top layer shorter than the bottom, the opening for the arm between the two. This gown is usually made in substantial black fabric and is sometimes trimmed with velvet bands. Today vergers often wear standard academic gowns, perhaps with velvet bands on the sleeves.

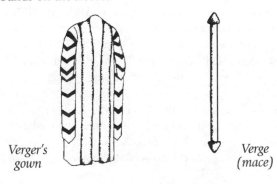

Verger's gown

Verge (mace)

A verger, robed, carries a **mace**, a "verge" or rod, when leading a processssion or conducting any person or group of persons to stations in a church where they will perform liturgically. Readers, for example, may be conducted to the lectern or a homilist to the pulpit. The mace is the verger's emblem of authority to lead these people. Although vergers are popularly associated with cathedrals and bishops, any church may have a verger—and a verger may also serve in other capacities such as sacristan, sexton, or head usher.

Hats and Caps

Clerical headgear is varied; most styles have been around for centuries. Clergy may choose not to wear hats at all when vested. But if they desire a headcovering besides the hood of a black cape, any one of the following would be suitable to accompany choir vestments.

A **biretta** is a squared cap of stiffened black fabric with three "blades" and a pompon on top. The bladeless corner goes to the left—until one earns a doctorate and the fourth blade. A biretta may be worn in church or out of doors. A bishop's biretta is black with purple piping and pompon or all red or purple with a green lining.

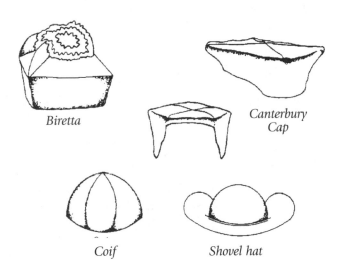

Biretta

Canterbury Cap

Coif

Shovel hat

A **square** or **Canterbury cap** is adapted from an academic mortarboard for outdoor wear. The "board" is loosely encased in black, and extended soft sides fit closely around the back of the head and the ears.

The shovel hat is also black and worn outdoors. The round crown is shallow and the brim wide, curving up all around.

Coif and **zuchetto** are two of the names for the skullcap sometimes worn in church during a service—red or purple for bishop, black for a priest.

CHAPTER 6

Special Occasions

*A*dvent, Christmas and Epiphany, Ash Wednesday, Palm Sunday, Holy Week and the Great Vigil of Easter, Easter itself and Pentecost—these days establish the rhythm of the church year. They are the common denominator of Christian liturgy. Some basic ceremonial for each occasion is set forth in the rubrics. But through the centuries certain other customs have become attached to these days, none of which are in the rubrics although they have become familiar patterns of parish liturgy. These patterns need remodeling, from time to time, refreshing in the light of the liturgical life of the whole church as well as the parish family.

An Advent wreath, a Christmas crèche, and representations of the three kings with gifts; ashes, the Lenten array but no flowers, and palm leaves marking the progress to the cross; foot washing, stations of the cross, and a three-hour watch; the new fire of Holy Saturday, the Paschal candle, Easter gardens, and red everywhere for Pentecost—all these extra customs are in the realm of altar guild work. They add to the already unusual preparation for special days—changed hangings, for example, different layouts for flowers and candles, festal vessels and linens. A creative altar guild with an eye to parish sensitivities and the approval of the priest is free to substitute others or to add more.

In addition to preparing for the days and seasons of the church year, an altar guild also prepares for Baptisms, weddings, and funerals; confirmations, ordinations at all levels of ministry, and all the other threshhold-crossing steps in the lives of parishioners and of the parish. Many of these special occasions are one-time events in the lives of the persons involved. It is important that these persons as well as the altar guild keep in mind that such occasions are first and foremost religious occasions, liturgical occasions. They have to be conducted and prepared for under the supervision of the rector of the parish within the bounds set by the rubrics in *The Book of Common Prayer* and sometimes by canon law as well. Individual requests can be addressed within those bounds.

Ultimately, liturgy grows out of the group that worships. What holds constant among parishes is the rite itself—certain words of worship, the outward and visible signs of the sacraments. What varies is ceremonial, including the preparation for it: how to set up for each occasion, how to decorate, what vestments to make ready, and how to take care of extra details. Local circumstances always determine this ceremonial; to that extent, liturgy is parochial. It is as parochial for these special occasions as it is for the daily ones, and parish guidelines are vital so that everyone will know beforehand exactly what has to be done. General manuals or manuals for other parishes or dioceses just won't work.

The degree to which Episcopal parishes can be parochial and still be alike is readily illustrated by the ways they celebrate the sacrament of marriage: the core doesn't move, but most of the periphery does![31] So it is with Baptisms and funerals/memorial services. Most brides and grooms, for example, "do" their weddings following their own patterns, but they marry within the framework provided by the Prayer Book. Carefully written parish "customaries" will simplify the preparation for these occasions. They will also provide printed answers to questions often raised about subjects that could lead to unnecessary controversy, such as acceptable flower placement and disposal, extra candles and special linens or vestments, photography during a service, even bird seed at the church door.

As altar guild members amass ideas about how to "do" weddings by attending weddings, so they amass ideas, a wealth of ideas, about how to prepare their own sacred spaces for all special occasions by visiting a variety of other parishes at these times. It is up to altar guild members to be the lookouts for their parish communities because other members of the communities seldom worship far afield. It is up to altar guild members also to gather ideas about ways to observe special days from books and from articles in church and altar guild publications.[32] The ideas are out there waiting to stimulate imaginations, to point to new patterns of preparing for worship. Introducing some of these patterns in a parish will lead the worshipers, the priest, and the altar guild, on a real adventure in new liturgical territory.

The Challenge

*G*od forever calls his people to worship him, to offer their lives at the altar, imperfect as they may be, to return to him the gifts he has given them. The worship of a parish family is this kind of offering, a gift of the parish life as it is at any time. The altar guild prepares for that worship.

The church has inherited certain ways of performing the central acts of formal worship, practices that spoke for other times and other places. *The New Altar Guild Book* describes some of the practices and furnishings of worship in the journey from yesterday into today. More background detail is included in this edition than was in the first because the remote yesterdays are now so much a part of current Episcopal liturgy. Being able to see the yesterdays as they were gives perspective to altar guild work as it is now and opens windows on its tomorrows. The continuing challenge to the church, to every parish of the church, is to explore new ways of carrying out the familiar actions here and now, wherever the here and now may be.

And the continuing challenge to every altar guild is to maintain a current set of guidelines that allows for this kind of exploration and at the same time covers the essential information altar guilds need in order to understand and carry out their ministry in their different places. *The New Altar Guild Book* is intended to give them the background to prepare such guidelines. It is intended to provide such an abundance of alternatives to choose among in preparing places for worship that they will absorb a sense of their freedom to develop their own patterns within the boundaries set by the rubrics. Many altar guilds have already written guidelines, parish manuals. Their continuing challenge is to keep rewriting them, updating them, adjusting them as liturgy changes. Altar guild members work in a today that their teachers could not have predicted on the edge of a tomorrow that they cannot forsee. Guidelines have to be written to be ready for that tomorrow in each place. This was not

97

always so, but it is now. And while preparing the church for worship may have been simpler and surer with the predictability of liturgy yesterday, it is certainly more interesting with the diversity of liturgy today!

Appendix 1

NATIONAL, PROVINCIAL, AND DIOCESAN ALTAR GUILD ORGANIZATION

The National Altar Guild Association is rooted in two organizations. First is a National Altar Guild Committee formed at General Convention in 1922 by a small group of altar guild leaders. Second is the National Association of Diocesan Altar Guilds (NADAG), an outgrowth of that Committee, formed at General Convention in 1961. Both groups worked to spread information about altar guild work, to fill mission needs in this country and overseas, to encourage and support diocesan altar guilds, and to be an altar guild presence at General Conventions with a corporate Communion and breakfast, an exhibit booth, and programs or workshops if possible. NADAG was a much larger group than the committee, but membership was confined to Diocesan Altar Guild directresses.

In 1987, at an interim meeting between Conventions, NADAG reorganized to become the National Altar Guild Association (NAGA) and to include in the membership altar guilds at all levels as well as individuals with altar guild background. NAGA's purpose, under its bylaws, is to unite all altar guilds and assist in organizing diocesan and provincial altar guilds; to serve as a two-way link between all altar guilds and the Presiding Bishop (to whom NAGA is responsible); to assist the national church in meeting its ecclesiastical and mission needs within the scope of the altar guild ministry, such as making stoles for chaplains of the armed forces; and to provide resources, information, and a newsletter. Every third year at the time and place of General Convention, NAGA meets as a whole, participating in an informative program, a corporate Communion, a public exhibit of pieces of ecclesiastical art submitted by the dioceses, a general business meeting, and the election of officers. (The names of current NAGA officers are listed in the *Episcopal Church Annual*, usually found in every parish office.)

In several provinces, leaders of diocesan altar guilds have formed

provincial altar guilds to further their basic purpose of relaying information and supporting each other's projects. They are loosely and differ-
ently organized, and are funded by diocesan dues and/or the province
budget. Through association in these groups, the leaders communicate in
person or by newsletters and arrange provincial altar guild meetings, perhaps once a year, for fellowship, worship, and exchange of information.
The Province I Altar Guild, formed in 1920, spearheaded the collection
of chaplains' supplies for the Army-Navy Commission during World War
II. Provincial altar guilds are represented on the NAGA board.

A diocesan altar guild is responsible to the bishop whom it serves.
Like parish and provincial altar guilds, these groups, too, have no set
pattern for organization. Usually but not always the president and any
other officers are appointed or at least approved by the bishop, and
the guild activities are subject to the bishop's approval. Some diocesan altar guilds are comprised of just an executive committee; others
include all parish altar guild leaders as well; still others include all altar
guild members in the diocese. In a few dioceses only one person is
appointed with the specified tasks of attending to diocesan events, to
non-parochial diocesan altars, and to the bishop's vestments and
other regalia. The ministry of most diocesan altar guilds stretches
beyond the above obligations to include at least some of these other
activities: newsletters; resource fairs; retreats; workshops for arranging
flowers, making linens and vestments, and creating needlepoint vesture and kneelers; a lending library for slides, videos, and books about
liturgy and ecclesiastical art; a diocesan "closet" for relocating used
church furnishings. It has increasingly become the practice for the
diocesan altar guild leader to serve on the diocesan liturgical committee. Most diocesan altar guilds meet at least once a year, usually with
the bishop, for a corporate Communion, instructive program, and fellowship. Most receive financial support for their projects from some
combination of voluntary contributions, dues, donations from the
Episcopal Church Women, and an allowance from the diocesan program budget. Names of diocesan altar guild presidents are also listed
in the *Episcopal Church Annual* under "Altar Guilds."

Forming a diocesan altar guild is possible when the bishop of a diocese and the altar guild members in that diocese both recognize the benefits of such an organization to the diocese on the one hand and to the
parish altar guilds on the other. It needs the support of both, not only
at the outset but on a continuing basis. When that support is present, a
diocesan altar guild has an effective ministry, often a very extensive one.

Appendix 2

A useful housekeeping sacristy has a sink big enough for cleaning and laundry tasks and also for working with the largest flower containers. It also has a **piscina**, a sink that drains directly onto the ground for rinsing vessels and linens that have been used in the Eucharist. If there is no piscina, a bowl may be substituted for this rinsing, the rinse water then being emptied onto the ground. If there is *only* a piscina, it is used just for vessels and linens, general sink work being done in another place. If there is no plumbing at all, water can be carried in for both rinsing and washing.

The useful sacristy has a counter space or a tabletop large enough for the guild's necessary work. Such work includes laying out vestments, if that is done (see "Vestments: What to Wear, When"), and spreading small laundered linens to dry (see linen section). The sacristy has mops, broom, vacuum cleaner, dustcloths, and similar housekeeping helpers; soaps, polishes, and other cleaning substances; towels and at least two dishpans—one for linens and vessels (preferably plastic to protect them), the other for general use. It has a comprehensive guide to spot removal and an assortment of basic aids for removing "church" stains. It has an ironing board and an iron for touchup pressing, even if regular ironing is done elsewhere. It has a church calendar, a clock, a wastebasket, and a full-length mirror; plain and padded hangers, tissue paper for padding and wrapping, and both cloth and plastic garment bags of necessary sizes. It has materials for any sewing emergency, including threads matching all the vestments in use, safety pins and common pins, sewing scissors, a tape measure, and a yardstick. It has a carton of matches, a box of tissues, and first-aid supplies including aspirin or the equivalent, bandages, first-aid spray, burn ointment, smelling salts, and cough drops; handy tools such as large scissors, tongs, screw driver, hammer, and paring knives;

101

and various containers, "mechanics," and tools for flower arranging—unless these are more conveniently stored in a separate place. The equivalent of desk space is desirable, not only for writing but for storing writing materials, altar guild instructions and books, the parish register, cards and a street map for altar flower delivery to homes and hospitals. A bulletin board for notices is important.

In addition to being well-equipped for housekeeping, a useful working sacristy provides storage spaces for *all* the items used in the worship life of the parish, from vestments and hangings, vessels and linens, candles and vases, bread (unless it is homemade) and wine, to the Christmas crèche, the Advent wreath, and wedding kneelers. An Episcopal Church uses an incredible amount of paraphernalia in its liturgy. It is up to the sacristy housekeepers to devise a way to store it all carefully and yet have it readily available!

Appendix 3

I nsurance companies as well as the National Altar Guild Association and diocesan business officers stress the need for exact records of *all* the materials and equipment that an altar guild has in custody. An inventory includes items in storage as well as those in current use.

A general list can be a helpful starting point, perhaps a list made from the descriptive lists included in the different sections of this book. As has already been said, however, all parishes have all the items in a general list (even in storage). Some have more, and most have others— their own treasures for special worship occasions. *Probably only the altar guild in a parish knows exactly what goods are its responsibility.* So the best method for a parish altar guild president or inventory committee to follow while preparing an inventory is to stand in the sacristy and systematically list the contents of each cupboard and drawer. Include whatever is hanging on the walls as well as stored items. Every item counts; remembering them away from the scene is not always satisfactory.

An inventory is both a business document to substantiate value when replacing items and a church record of parish property, in particular, memorial gifts. The two bodies of information may be recorded separately because an insurance company needs to know only the description and value of a chalice, for example, not who gave it in memory of whom! Any such document requires a date. For each item, record the *quantity;* a *meticulous description,* including blemishes as well as embellishments; *replacement value;* the *manner of acquisition* (purchase? made by the altar guild? or gift from whom?); *date acquired;* if a *memorial,* to whom from whom; *ownership* (parish? priest? or other?).

A photographic inventory is just as important as a written one, not only for proof of ownership and evaluation, but for parish

103

history. Photograph each item individually and in color—vessels, linens, vestments, hangings, brasses, crosses, torches, woodcarvings, statues, other artwork, needlepoint. Don't overlook anything! Include a measure in each photograph to verify the size. Photograph fronts and backs, embroideries, engravings, other ornamentation, hallmarks, legends, labels, signatures, blemishes— whatever sets the item apart from all others. In an album with treated plastic pages, place each photograph accompanied by a card with a written description containing all the information listed above. Make three copies of the photographs and the written information—one set to go in the safe deposit box, one in the lawyer's vault, and one in the sacristy for regular updating.

Appendix 4

*T*he common stains that altar guilds encounter are wine, lipstick, soot, scorch, mildew, blood, rust, and candle wax. The sooner any of these stains is treated, the easier its removal. Including a stain-removal chart in a parish altar guild manual, or posting it where altar guild workers can easily refer to it, is a good idea. So is keeping on hand in the sacristy a supply of the common products used in stain removal, with directions for use.

In general, simple, even old-fashioned, methods are best. Alcohol, ammonia, club soda, 3 percent peroxide, table salt, turpentine, and, of course, cold water, boiling water, lemon juice, and white soap are all useful and effective home remedies for different spots, gentler than many commercial spot-removal agents. Every housekeeper has preferred ways for removing specific stains; so do the different authors of books about stain removal. So do altar guild members—and all are usually more than ready to share! Questions about stains invariably arise at altar guild conferences and are a frequent subject in altar guild newsletters. The suggestions that follow are only a sample of the information available on this subject. These all work, but others undoubtedly work equally well.

Blood

A blood stain disappears when sponged immediately with the saliva of the person whose blood it is. A bit of spit and a rub with the finger or a piece of white cloth, and the stain is gone! Otherwise soak a fresh blood stain in several changes of cold water and then wash with white soap. Soak a *set* blood spot in a half-and-half solution of 3 percent peroxide and ammonia, and then wash.

Candle-wax

On wood or stone, glass or plastic: Soften the wax with a hair dryer, wipe the wax away with an absorbent paper towel, and rinse the surface with a solution of vinegar and water. Scraping the wax will scratch the object.

On unlacquered brass and other metals: Work with a separate bowl so waxy water won't cling to the sink or clog the drain. (Adding tri-sodium phosphate, TSP, to the water in the bowl prevents both problems.) Pour boiling water over the article or immerse the article in it and swirl. Wipe the article immediately with a paper towel. Repeat if necessary.

On lacquered brass and other metals: Use the hair dryer method, but don't rinse with vinegar. Just wipe.

On linen: Remove excess wax by scraping gently with a dull implement like the back of a knife. Chill the article first in the freezer to facilitate the scraping. Pour a small amount of turpentine onto the spot, then wash with soap and water. The odor will dissipate and the residual stain should disappear. Or pour boiling water through the spot from a height, then rub with a degreasing detergent and wash. Or place the waxy spot in a sandwich of white blotters or brown paper (not paper towels) and iron it with a moderately hot iron. The paper should absorb the wax. Repeat with fresh blotters if necessary. Sponge any residual stain with alcohol, or salt and lemon juice, or turpentine, or detergent, or a commercial degreaser—and wash as usual.

On cloth other than linen: The blotter and iron method works on many materials, but not all. Understand the fabric to be treated. If in doubt, consult a reputable dry cleaner.

On carpets: Use the blotter and iron method, placing the blotter on the wax. Repeat with fresh blotters if necessary. Sponge any residual stain with cleaning fluid.

Candle oil from most oil candles will *not* stain. If it spills on vestments, hangings, or linen, simply let it dry.

Holy oil (which is olive oil) *will* stain vestments if the priest's thumb touches the cloth. Apply dry or slightly dampened corn starch to the stain and let it sit for about half a day. Then brush off with a clean firm toothbrush. To forestall holy oil stains on vestments, provide lemon wedges as well as water for the priest's hand washing after anointing.

Lipstick
Apply a degreasing laundry detergent directly to the spot and

106

rub gently until the spot disappears. Then rinse. Some lipstick colors are stubborn, so repeating the process may be necessary. For really difficult lipstick stains, use 3 percent peroxide and ammonia, mixed half and half, on washable white material and cleaning fluid on nonwashables.

Mildew

Light mildew can usually be removed from washables by laundering with soap and water, rinsing well, and drying in the sun spread flat on the grass. If this doesn't work, repeat—but soak in 3 percent peroxide first. Dry-clean nonwashables. Heavy mildew may prove impossible to remove.

Rust

Cover stain with cream of tartar and immerse it in hot water for five minutes, then wash. Or moisten the stain, sprinkle it with salt, wet it thoroughly with lemon juice, and let it dry in the sun, spread flat on the grass.

Scorch

For non-washables, soak a press cloth with peroxide, lay it over the stain, and iron with a warm iron. For all colorfast washables, sponge stain with peroxide and wash.

Soot, Ashes, and Smoke

For washables, rub liquid detergent into the stain and rinse well. Repeat if necessary. Sponge non-washables with cleaning fluid until the stain disappears. If a trace remains, rub it with synthetic detergent and rinse.

Wine

When the stain is fresh, soak *immediately* in club soda for several minutes, rub gently, and rinse. The wine should disappear. *Note:* Club soda applied generously to blot out the stain may be effective on vestments and needlepoint if the stain is fresh, but generally non-washables with wine stains should be dry-cleaned. For washables, when the stain is not fresh, sprinkle it with salt and pour boiling water through it from a height until it disappears *or* sprinkle it with salt, immerse it in cold water, and rub the stain out.

Appendix 5

*T*he following list of books about church needlework contains only a tiny fraction of what has been written on the subject. Some of these books and many more are available in general bookstores, church bookstores, and public libraries. Look for books about the many aspects of church needlework in the more specialized libraries and bookstores maintained by cathedrals and conference centers, convents and monasteries, and some museums. The National Altar Guild Association lists many titles in its library (send inquiries to the president). Several church suppliers and publishers offer a good selection. If a book is currently out of print, don't give up the search. Updated editions periodically appear. And on occasion a sought-after old edition will turn up in a collection of second-hand books—a real find!

Banbury, Gisela and Dewar, Angela, *How to Design and Make Banners* (Harrisburg: Morehouse Publishing, 1992). Step-by-step instructions from start to finish. Good illustrations.

Dean, Beryl, *Church Needlework*. Also *Ecclesiastical Embroidery; Embroidery for Religion and Ceremonial; Ideas for Church Embroidery* (London: B.T. Batsford, 1980s.). Acclaimed as the foremost authority in the field. Fascinating, informative descriptions and pictures of projects.

Edwards, Joan, *Church Kneelers* (Dorking, Surrey, England: Bayford Books, 1967). A small concise book for beginners. Her instructions are meticulous, her designs contemporary. Can be used as a single reference.

Ford, Karen, "Ecclesiastical Designs in Needlework," a very useful catalog. Tremendous assortment of needlework aids including excellent books. P.O.Box 15178, Phoenix, Arizona, 85060.

Ireland, Marion P., *Textile Art in the Church* (Abingdon Press, 1980). Excellent total reference for all church needlework. A must-see classic!

Jerdee, Rebecca, *Appliqué for Worship: Patterns and Guide for Sewing Banners, Vestments, and Paraments* (Augsburg-Fortress, 1982).

Joseph, Elizabeth, *Sewing Church Linens* (Harrisburg, PA: Morehouse Publishing, 1991). Contemporary approach to convent work. Based on extensive experience teaching inexperienced parish altar guild women to make all their own linens successfully. Large clear diagrams for each step in the process, excellent designs for embroidery, and careful but informal text.

Mackrille, Lucy Vaughan Hayden, *Church Embroidery and Church Vestments* (Chevy Chase, MD: Cathedral Studios. Inquire: Altar Guild, National Cathedral, Mt. St. Alban's, Washington, DC). A complete and practical guide to this craft as it was mid-century; a 1939 classic still useful in the nineties. Basic. Many designs and illustrations. Worth hunting for.

McNeill, Lucy, *Sanctuary Linens: Choosing, Making, and Embroidering* (Toronto: Anglican Book Centre, 600 Jarvis St. M2Y4J6, 1975). A good reference for any level of experience! Excellent illustrations.

Olsen, Mary, *For the Greater Glory* (New York: Seabury Press, 1980). An outstanding all-inclusive contemporary book on needlepoint for the church.

Post, Willard Ellwood, *Saints, Signs, and Symbols*, 2nd edition (Harrisburg, PA: Morehouse Publishing, 1990). A classic on this subject for years. Large line drawings of just about any church symbol with text about each.

Raynor, Louise H. and Kerr, Carolyn A., *Church Needlepoint*, 2nd edition (Harrisburg, PA: Morehouse Publishing, 1989). A small, basic book with simple designs and easy steps. Very good for beginners.

Reynolds, Nancy, compiler, *Needlepoint Kneelers, A Collection of Religious Symbolism*. Over four hundred pictures of the kneelers of Christ Church Christiana Hundred, Wilmington, Delaware. A display of symbolism in this art as complete as any that exists, with text about each symbol. Excellent reference book, worth the price. Available from Christ Church.

Appendix 6

A Vested Chalice

1. The Chalice
2. Purificator
3. The Paten
4. The Priest's Wafer (optional)
5. Linen Pall
6. Silk Veil
7. Burse

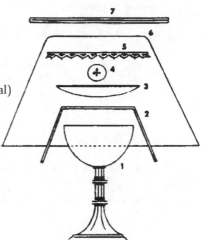

Eucharist Vestments

1. Chasuble
2. Maniple
3. Stole
4. Girdle
5. Alb
6. Amice

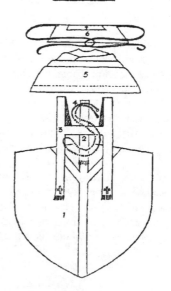

Notes

1. *Constitution & Canons for the Government of the Protestant Episcopal Church in the United States of America otherwise known as The Episcopal Church Adopted in General Convention 1789-1994.* TITLE III, CANON 14. Sec. 1.(a): "The authority of and responsibility for the conduct of the worship and the spiritual jurisdiction of the Parish are vested in the Rector subject to the Rubrics of the Book of Common Prayer, the Constitution and Canons of the Church, and the pastoral direction of the Bishop." And (c): "For the purpose of the office and for the full and free discharge of all functions and duties pertaining thereto, the Rector shall at all times be entitled to the use and control of the Church and Parish buildings with the appurtenances and furniture thereof." And (d): "In a Missionary Cure, the control and responsibility belong to the Priest who has been duly appointed to the charge thereof, subject to the authority of the Bishop."

2. Dom Gregory Dix, *The Shape of the Liturgy* (London: dacre press, 1964), 421.

3. John Baillie, *Diary of Private Prayer* (New York: Chas. Scribner and Sons, 1949), 63.

4. Percy Dearmer, *The Parson's Handbook* (Milwaukee, WI: Young Churchman, 1903), 172, 173.

5. Marion J. Hatchett, *Sanctifying Life, Time, and Space* (New York: Seabury Press, 1976), chap. 8 passim, especially 145, 151-59.

6. W. Appleton Lawrence, *Parsons, Vestries, and Parishes* (Greenwich, CT: Seabury Press, 1961), 183.

7. Lawrence, *Parsons*, 184.

8. For further information about church furnishings, hangings, and lights, consult Percy Dearmer, Dom Gregory Dix, and Marion Hatchett (as noted above) and J.G. Davies, ed., *Westminster Dictionary of Worship* (Philadelphia: Westminster Press, 1972).

9. Dearmer, *Parson's Handbook*, 146.

10. Dix, *Liturgy*, 418.

11. Hatchett, *Sanctifying*, 158; and Dearmer, *Parson's Handbook*, 97.

12. Excellent books about conditioning and arranging flowers for altars are *Flowers to the Glory of God* (Keedysville, MD: Fellfoot Publishers, 1990) and *Homage Through Flowers* (Glen Burnie, MD: French/Bray Printing, 1978), both by Sandra Hynson, former Head of the Washington Cathedral Altar Guild and leader of countless workshops on this subject. If these books are unavailable elsewhere, send inquiry to Head of the Altar Guild, Washington Cathedral, Mt. St. Alban's, Washington, DC. Many church-oriented libraries list these books. Another helpful book on this subject is Jean Taylor, *Flowers in Church* (Harrisburg, PA: Morehouse Publishing, 1985).

13. Improvised containers that have been used because they "worked" for a specific occasion or location run the gamut from washtubs to tuna fish cans, old bottles to crystal goblets. The best flower arrangers don't let the mechanics show unless the mechanics enhance the arrangement.

14. The principal references for this section are Dom Gregory Dix, *The Shape of the Liturgy*, chaps. 1-6 and passim; Marion Hatchett, *Commentary on the American Prayer Book* (New York: Seabury Press, 1981), 289-308 and passim; and Massey Shepherd, all three books listed in the bibliography.

15. *The First and Second Prayer Books of Edward VI*, Everyman's Library (New York: E.P. Dutton, Inc, 1957), 230 and 392.

16. National Altar Guild Association meeting, Phoenix, Arizona, July 1991.

17. National Altar Guild Association meeting, Detroit, Michigan, July, 1988.

18. Hatchett, *A Manual of Ceremonial for the New Prayer Book* (Sewanee, TN: School of Theology, University of the South, 1977), 10.

19. H. Boone Porter, Jr., retired professor of liturgics, General Theological Seminary, correspondence.

20. The principal references for vestments are Cyril Pocknee, *Liturgical Vesture, Its Origins and Development* (London: A.R. Mowbray, 1960);

Westminster Dictionary of Worship; Percy Dearmer, *Parson's Handbook*; and Christie C. Mayer-Thurman, *Raiment for the Lord's Service: A Thousand Years of Western Vestments* (Chicago: Art Institute, 1975).

21. *Westminster Dictionary of Worship*, 380.

22. Charles P. Price and Louis Weil, *Liturgy for Living* (New York: Seabury Press, 1979), 90.

23. Mayer-Thurman, *Raiment for the Lord's Service*.

24. The Merrimac River Valley Textile Museum (North Andover, MA) is one such museum. St. John Baptist Convent (Mendham, NJ) and C.M. Almy & Sons (Greenwich, CT) are good resources.

25. Sources differ slightly in recording the history of different vestments, and creators of today's versions of the different types also differ slightly in their decisions about what will be useful and attractive. Difference in vestments is as natural as difference in any other class of clothing. The first cassock-alb was made about twenty-five years ago, for example, and today several different versions of the one garment are shown. The descriptions of vestments in this book are more or less standard, based on Pocknee, *Liturgical Vesture*; *Westminster Dictionary*; the Holyrood Guild "Notes"; and a variety of catalogs from vestment suppliers.

26. *Westminster Dictionary*, 368.

27. *Westminster Dictionary*, 375.

28. Pocknee, *Liturgical Vesture*, 48.

29. Ibid., 43.

30. Kenneth Walter Cameron, ed., *The Church of England in Pre-Revolutionary Connecticut* (Hartford, CT: Transcendental Books, 1976), letter from Chas. Inglis to Samuel Seabury, 235.

31. In 1985 the authors surveyed "marriage booklets" from approximately seventy-five parishes in different areas of the United States. These booklets were local manuals for all those involved in "putting on" a wedding. A few focused only on preparing for the service itself. But most covered all the church-related steps along the way, from filing intentions at the parish office to leaving the church as husband and wife (or the parish house after a church reception). Almost no point was left in question, and almost every booklet was in some

aspect different from the others. Copies of the report on this survey are available from the authors.

32. Among the books of suggestions are H. Boone Porter, Jr., *Keeping the Church Year* (New York: Seabury Press, 1977); Marion J.Hatchett, *Commentary on the American Prayer Book* (New York: Seabury Press, 1981); and Byron D. Stuhlman, *Prayer Book Rubrics Expanded* (New York: Church Hymnal Corporation, 1987). Related articles also appear regularly in church-oriented publications such as altar guild newsletters; *Open*, the journal of the Associated Parishes for Liturgy and Mission (Fort Worth, TX) and that organization's several brochures on parish life and worship; and *The Living Church*.

Bibliography

The following books, printouts of lectures, and altar guild manuals are those used as background in writing this book. Most are old friends from the time of writing the first edition, now revisited. A few have been added. The liturgical transition that all Episcopalians have been experiencing in recent years burst into print in the middle of the twentieth century through the effort of men and women deeply involved in liturgy, both studying it and doing it. They wrote most of these books, sharing their wisdom. They were the adventurers in the new territory that we now are settling.

The Book of Common Prayer According to the Use of the Episcopal Church. New York: Church Hymnal Corporation, 1979.

Booty, John E. *The Church in History.* New York: Seabury Press, 1979.

Buckland, Patricia B. *Advent to Pentecost: A History of the Christian Year.* Wilton, CT: Morehouse-Barlow, 1977.

Cameron, Kenneth Walter, ed. *The Church of England in Pre-Revolutionary Connecticut.* Hartford, CT: Transcendental Books, 1976.

Davies, J.G., ed. *The Westminster Dictionary of Worship.* Philadelphia: Westminster Press, 1972.

Dearmer, Percy. *The Parson's Handbook.* Milwaukee, WI: Young Churchman, 1903.

Dix, Gregory. *The Shape of the Liturgy.* London: dacre press, 1964.

Edwards, O.C. *How It All Began.* New York: Seabury Press, 1973.

Evans, H. Barry, ed. *Prayer Book Renewal.* New York: Seabury Press, 1978.

First and Second Prayer Books of Edward VI. Everyman's Library. New York: E.P. Dutton, 1957.

Hatchett, Marion J. "The Holy Eucharist," in *Commentary on the American Prayer Book*, 289-422. New York: Seabury Press, 1981.

_____ *A Manual of Ceremonial for the New Prayer Book*. Sewanee, TN: School of Theology, University of the South, 1977.

_____ *Sanctifying Life, Time, and Space: An Introduction to Liturgical Study*. New York: Seabury Press, 1976.

Holmes, Urban T. *The Future Shape of Ministry*. New York: Seabury Press, 1971.

Hovda, Robert. *Strong, Loving, and Wise: Presiding in Liturgy*. Washington DC: Liturgical Conference, 1984.

Hynson, Sandra S. *Homage Through Flowers: A Handbook*. Glen Burnie, MD: French/Bray Printing, 1978.

_____ *Flowers to the Glory of God: A Handbook*. Keedysville, MD: Felfoot Publishers, 1990.

Jones, Cheslyn; Wainwright, Geoffrey; and Yarnold, Edward; eds. *The Study of Liturgy*. New York: Oxford University Press, 1978.

Kay, Melissa, editor. *It Is Your Own Ministry*. Washington, DC: Liturgical Conference, ca 1980.

Ladd, William Palmer. *Prayer Book Interleaves*. New York: Oxford University Press, 1943.

Lawrence, William Appleton. Chap. 15 in *Parsons, Vestries, and Parishes: A Manual*. Greenwich, CT: Seabury Press, 1961.

Mayer-Thurman, Christie C. *Raiment for the Lord's Service: A Thousand Years of Western Vestments*. Chicago: Art Institute, 1975.

Micks, Marianne. *The Future Present*. New York: Seabury Press, 1977.

_____ *The Joy of Worship*. New York: Seabury Press, 1980.

Pocknee, Cyril E. *Liturgical Vesture, Its Origin and Development*. Alcuin Club Tracts XXX. London: A.R. Mowbray, 1960.

Porter, H. Boone, Jr. *Keeping the Church Year*. New York: Seabury Press, 1977.

Pregnall, William S. *Laity and Liturgy: A Handbook for Parish Worship.* New York: Seabury Press, 1975.

Price, Charles P. *Introducing the Proposed Book.* New York: Church Hymnal Corporation, 1976.

Price, Charles P., and Weil, Louis. *Liturgy for Living.* New York: Seabury Press, 1979.

Rodenmayer, Robert N. *Thanks Be To God.* New York: Harper and Brothers, 1960.

Schmemann, Alexander. *Liturgy and Life: Christian Development through Liturgical Experience.* New York: Department of Religious Education, Orthodox Church in America, 1974.

Shepherd, Massey Hamilton, Jr. *At All Times and In All Places.* New York: Seabury Press, 1965.

_____ *The Liturgical Renewal of the Church.* New York: Oxford University Press, 1960.

_____ *The Reform of Liturgical Worship.* New York: Oxford University Press, 1961.

Smith, Charles W.F., ed. *A Prayer Book Manual.* Arlington, VA: Evangelical Education Society, 1981.

Standing Liturgical Commission of the Protestant Episcopal Church in the United States of America. *Prayer Book Studies IV: The Eucharistic Liturgy.* New York: Church Pension Fund, 1953.

Stuhlman, Byron D. *Prayer Book Rubrics Expanded.* New York: Church Hymnal Corporation, 1987.

Taylor, Jean. *Flowers in Church.* Harrisburg, PA: Morehouse Publishing, 1985.

Associated Parishes for Liturgy and Mission. Brochures on parish life and worship: *The Daily Office; Celebrating Redemption; The Great Vigil of Easter; The Catechumenate; Holy Baptism: Parish Eucharist; The Holy Eucharist, Rite II; The Celebration and Blessing of a Marriage; The Burial of the Dead; Holy Orders; The Parish Worship Committee; Ministry I: Holy Baptism; Ministry II: Laity, Bishops, Priests and Deacons.* Alexandria, VA: Associated Parishes, 1976-91. (Statement at the beginning of each pamphlet:

"The Associated Parishes for Liturgy and Mission is a group of persons belonging to the Episcopal Church, the Anglican Church of Canada, and other Christian Churches, who are committed to the renewal of Christian life and worship. During almost half a century, since 1946, this group has concerned itself especially with providing an articulate expression of the principles of the liturgical movement in North America, as these have been experienced and tested within the lives of our congregations.")

ALTAR GUILD MANUALS
(ARRANGED IN CHRONOLOGICAL ORDER OF ORIGINAL PUBLICATION.)

Smart, Rev. Henry. *The Altar: Its Ornaments and Its Care.* Milwaukee, WI: Morehouse Publishing Co., 1925.

Perry, Edith Weir. *An Altar Guild Manual.* Rev. ed. New York: Morehouse-Barlow, 1963.

McClinton, Katherine Morrison, and Squier, Isabel Wright. *Good Housekeeping in the Church.* New York: Morehouse-Gorham, 1951.

Diggs, Dorothy C. *A Working Manual for Altar Guilds.* Rev. ed. New York: Morehouse-Barlow, 1973.

Altar Guild Manuals, original and revised, of the dioceses of Dallas, Connecticut, Oklahoma, and Minnesota.

Hatchett, Marion J., and LeCroy, Anne K. *The Altar Guild Handbook.* San Francisco: Harper & Row, Publishers, 1986.

Taylor, B. Don. *The Complete Training Course for Altar Guilds.* Harrisburg, PA: Morehouse Publishing, 1993.

(In addition to these published manuals, the authors have, since 1982, read through numbers of "loose-leaf" manuals newly created by parish altar guilds across the United States. The diversity among them supports the premise of this book—that each situation calls for its own process of preparing sacred space in which to worship God.)